Host Country Impact Study:
Armenia

TABLE OF CONTENTS

LIST OF TABLES

LIST OF FIGURES

ACKNOWLEDGEMENTS[1]

Several people at Peace Corps/headquarters were instrumental in launching the pilot studies in the impact evaluation series. Three regional program and training advisers, Barbara Brown, Michael McCabe, and Margaret McLaughlin, shepherded the studies from initial concept to implementation in their regions. The country desk officers and sector specialists, Jason Burns, Dawn Hodge, Frances Kambour, Nicole Lewis, Frank Smith, and Peggy Seufert, provided the crucial link between OSIRP researchers and the posts. Thank you.

The interest and support from Peace Corps staff in the countries where the research was conducted were critical in this endeavor. Our sincere appreciation is extended to country directors Lee Lacy, Armenia; Romeo Massey, Dominican Republic; and Michael Simsik, Mali; and their staff: Jason Compy, Diana Sargsyan, and Gayane Zargaryan in Armenia; Martina Barinas, Miguel Leon, and Tamara Simo in the Dominican Republic; and Seydou Coulibaly in Mali. The OSIRP team is especially appreciative of the contributions provided by Dr. Romeo Massey during the initial design phase of the research.

The success of the studies is ultimately due to the work of the local research teams that skillfully encouraged the partners[2] of Peace Corps Volunteers to share their experiences and perspectives. The teams were headed by senior researchers Zhirayr Edilyan in Armenia, Jose Ricardo Roques in the Dominican Republic, and Mamadou Diallo in Mali.

---

[1] Although these studies were a team effort by all members of the OSIRP staff, we would like to recognize Susan Jenkins for her role as the study lead.

[2] Partners include any individuals who may have lived or worked with a Peace Corps Volunteer.

ACRONYMS AND DEFINITIONS

Acronyms

APCD	Assistant Peace Corp Director
BN	Beneficiary
CAMP GLOW	Girls Leading Our World Camp
CDPF	Civic Development and Partnership Foundation
CP	Counterpart
FLEX	Future Leaders Exchange Program
GOA	Government of Armenia
HCN	Host Country National
HF	Host Family
IST	In-Service Training
NGO	Non-Governmental Organization
OSIRP	Office of Strategic Information, Research and Planning
PC/A	Peace Corps/Armenia
PCV	Peace Corps Volunteer
PDM	Project Design and Management
TEFL	Teaching English as a Foreign Language
UGRAD	Global Undergraduate Exchange Program

Definitions

Beneficiaries	Individuals who receive assistance and help from the project; the people that the project is primarily designed to advantage
Counterparts/Project partners	Individuals who work with Peace Corps Volunteers; Volunteers may work with multiple partners and counterparts during their service. Project partners also benefit from the projects, but when they are paired with Volunteers in a professional relationship or based on their position in an

organization or community (e.g., community leader), they are considered counterparts or project partners

Host family members Families with whom a Volunteer lived during all or part of his/her training and/or service

Project stakeholders People who have a major involvement in the design, implementation or results of the project

EXECUTIVE SUMMARY

Introduction

In 2008, the Peace Corps launched a series of studies to determine the impact of Volunteers on two of the agency's three goals: building local capacity and promoting a better understanding of Americans among host country nationals (HCNs). The Peace Corps conducts an annual survey that captures the perspective of currently serving Volunteers.[3] While providing critical insight into the Volunteer experience, the survey can only address one side of the Peace Corps' story. The host country impact studies are unique for their focus on learning about the Peace Corps' impact directly from host country nationals who lived and worked with Volunteers.

This report presents the findings from the pilot study which was conducted in Armenia during the summer and fall of 2008. The focus of the research was the English Language Education Project.

Purpose of the Host Country Impact Studies

Armenia's Host Country Impact Study was initiated to assess the degree to which the Peace Corps is able to both meet the needs of the country in developing English language capacities and to promote a better understanding of Americans among host country nationals. The study will also allow the Peace Corps to have a better picture of the English Language Education Project and address areas where it could be improved.

The impact study documents the HCN perspective on the impact of Peace Corps Volunteers (PCVs) on skills transfer to and capacity building of host country counterparts and community members and on changes in host country nationals' understanding of Americans.

The major research questions addressed in the study are:

- Did skills transfer and capacity building occur?
- What skills were transferred to organizations/communities and individuals as a result of Volunteers' work?
- Were the skills and capacities sustained past the end of the project?
- How satisfied were HCNs with the project work?
- What did HCNs learn about Americans?
- Did HCNs report that their opinions of Americans had changed after interacting with the Peace Corps and Peace Corps Volunteers?

---

[3]Peace Corps surveyed Volunteers periodically from 1973 to 2002 when a biennial survey was instituted. The survey became an annual survey in 2009 to meet agency reporting requirements.

Evaluation Methodology

This evaluation report is based on data provided by counterparts, beneficiaries, and stake-holders of the English Language Education Project, including:

- 26 school-based counterparts (co-teachers)
- 22 beneficiaries (students)
- 24 host family members
- 4 Ministry officials
- 2 non-governmental organization (NGO) staff
- 10 exchange students

The overall survey reached 88 respondents in 24 rural and urban communities in four of Armenia's Marzes: Lori, Shirak, Syunik, and Gegharkunik.

Interviews were conducted from August 14 to November 13, 2009. (A full description of the methodology is found in Appendix 1. Please contact OSIRP for a copy of the interview questionnaire.)

The evaluation studies are designed by Peace Corps/headquarters' Office of Strategic Information, Research and Planning (OSIRP) and were implemented in-country by the Armenian firm, Civic Development and Partnership Foundation (CDPF).

Project Design and Purpose

The Peace Corps began sending Peace Corps Volunteers to Armenia in 1992 and the English Language Education Project was one of the first projects. The goal was to assist Armenia in enhancing its participation in the international community by increasing the quality of English programs and providing other educational opportunities throughout the country.

Evaluation Findings

The evaluation findings confirm the successful implementation of the English Language Education Project by Peace Corps/Armenia (PC/A). While the report provides a detailed description of all the study questions, the key findings are:

Goal 1 Findings

Successful Transfer of English Language Skills and Teaching Methods

- Improvement in English language proficiency and teaching skills were the most frequently mentioned individual-level changes
- Adoption of new teaching/classroom methods was the most frequently mentioned organizational change

Capacity Building was Sustained

- 92% of school-based projects were maintained after the Volunteer left (62% "to a large extent")
- 80% of community-based activities were maintained "to a small extent"

Satisfaction with Peace Corps Work

- 88% of counterparts were satisfied with the changes in their school as a result of the Peace Corps' work
- 76% of counterparts were very satisfied with the level of collaboration between their school and the Peace Corps
- 82% of counterparts reported that the Peace Corps' work met their schools' needs

Goal 2 Findings

HCNs Developed More Positive Opinions of Americans

- 71% of counterparts reported that their opinions of Americans improved after working with a Volunteer
- 97% of counterparts had a positive opinion of the Peace Corps as a result of their experiences
- 66% of host families rated their relationships with Volunteers positively

CHAPTER 1: INTRODUCTION

Background

The Peace Corps traces its roots and mission to 1960, when then-Senator John F. Kennedy challenged students at the University of Michigan to serve their country in the cause of peace by living and working in developing countries. From that inspiration grew an agency of the federal government devoted to world peace and friendship.

By the end of 1961, Peace Corps Volunteers were serving in seven countries. Since then, more than 200,000 men and women have served in 139 countries. Peace Corps activities cover issues ranging from AIDS education to information technology and environmental preservation. Peace Corps Volunteers continue to help countless individuals who want to build a better life for themselves, their children, and their communities.

In carrying out the agency's three core goals, Peace Corps Volunteers make a difference by building local capacity and promoting a better understanding of Americans among host country nationals. A major contribution of Peace Corps Volunteers, who live in the communities where they work, stems from their ability to deliver technical interventions directly to beneficiaries living in rural or urban areas that lack sufficient local capacity. Also, Volunteers operate from a development principle that promotes sustainable projects and strategies.

> ### Peace Corps' Core Goals
>
> **Goal 1**- To help the people of interested countries in meeting their need for trained men and women.
>
> **Goal 2**- To help promote a better understanding of Americans on the part of the peoples served.
>
> **Goal 3**- To help promote a better understanding of other people on the part of Americans.

The interdependence of Goal 1 and Goal 2 is central to the Peace Corps experience, as HCNs develop relationships with Volunteers who communicate in the local language, share everyday experiences, and work collaboratively.

The Peace Corps conducts an annual survey of currently serving Volunteers[4]; however, it tells only one side of the Peace Corps' story. In 2008, the Peace Corps began a series of studies to determine the impact of its Volunteers. The studies are unique for their focus on learning about the Peace Corps' impact directly from the host country nationals who lived and worked with Volunteers.

---

[4]Peace Corps surveyed Volunteers periodically from 1973 to 2002 when a biennial survey was instituted. The survey became an annual survey in 2009 to meet agency reporting requirements.

History of the Peace Corps/Armenia English Language Education Project

Peace Corps/Armenia began in September 1992, with the signing of an agreement between the Peace Corps and the Government of the Republic of Armenia. Later, a Memorandum of Understanding was signed between the Peace Corps and the Armenian Ministry of Science and Education to provide a framework for the English Language Education Project in Armenia. The goal of the English Language Education Project is to improve English language teaching and learning in the education sector and to increase the professional quality of English language teachers.

Purpose of the Host Country Impact Studies

This report presents the findings from the pilot impact evaluation conducted in Armenia during the summer and fall of 2008. The project studied was the English Language Education Project.

The impact study documents the HCN perspective on the impact of Peace Corps Volunteers on skills transfer to and capacity building of host country counterparts and community members and on changes in host country nationals' understanding of Americans.

The major research questions addressed in the study are:

- Did skills transfer and capacity building occur?
- What skills were transferred to organizations/communities and individuals as a result of Volunteers' work?
- Were the skills and capacities sustained past the end of the project?
- How satisfied were HCNs with the project work?
- What did HCNs learn about Americans?
- Did HCNs report that their opinions of Americans had changed after interacting with the Peace Corps and Peace Corps Volunteers?

The information gathered through this research will help the Peace Corps answer questions about the degree to which the agency is able—across posts, sectors, and sites—to meet the needs of host countries for trained men and women and to promote a better understanding of Americans among HCNs. This information complements the information provided by Peace Corps Volunteers in their Project Status Reports and the Annual Volunteer Survey.

Evaluation Methodology

In 2008, the Peace Corps' Office of Strategic Information, Research and Planning (OSIRP), in response to a mandate from the Office of Management and Budget that the agency should conduct evaluations of the impact of Volunteers in achieving Goal 2, began a series of evaluation studies. Armenia was one of three countries selected to pilot a methodology that would examine the impact of the technical work of Volunteers, as well as their efforts topromote a better understanding of Americans among the people with whom they served. In collaboration with the Peace Corps' country director at each post, OSIRP piloted a methodology to collect information *directly from host country nationals* about skills transfer and capacity building, as well as changes in their understanding of Americans.

The research was designed by OSIRP social scientists and implemented in-country by Zhirayr Edilyan and a team of interviewers, under the supervision of the Peace Corps' country staff, with technical direction from the OSIRP team. A web-based database was used to manage the questionnaire data and subsequent analysis.

In Armenia, the CDPF conducted interviews in 24 communities where Volunteers worked. Sixty-two English Language Education Project Volunteer site placements between 2004 and 2008 were identified for possible participation in the study. A representative sample rather than a random sample was drawn from the list of Volunteer assignments since 2004. Armenian Senior Researcher Edilyan and his team conducted semi-structured interviews with Armenians who had lived and/or worked with Peace Corps Volunteers. (The interview schedule is available upon request from OSIRP)

The overall survey reached 97 respondents in 24 rural and urban communities in four of Armenia's Marzes: Lori, Shirak, Syunik, and Gegharkunik. Sites were selected to be as representative of Armenia as possible, including geographic and socio-economic differences. The regions represent diverse population centers, ranging from small villages of 600 people to larger cities with a population of 150,000. (Appendix 1 contains a full description of the research methodology.)

Interviews were conducted from August 14 to November 13, 2008 with the following groups of Armenian nationals:

- **Project partners/counterparts**: Co-teachers, school administrators, and teacher supervisors (26)

- **Project beneficiaries**: University, college and secondary school students taught/co-taught by PCVs, and camp attendees (21)

- **Alumni of exchange programs**: Including programs such as FLEX, UGrad, and Muskie with whom Volunteers had worked to support their applications to these programs (10)

- **Staff of two non-governmental organizations**: Representatives of organizations with whom PCVs worked (2)

- **Host family members:** Families that hosted Volunteers during at least part of their service (24)

- **Stakeholders**: Representatives from the Ministry for Education and Science (3) and the National Institute of Education (1)

Interviewers recorded the respondents' comments, coded the answers, and then entered the data into a web-based database maintained by OSIRP. The data were analyzed by OSIRP researchers and the senior researcher.

Table 1: Number and Type of Host Country Nationals Interviewed: Armenia

Categories	Number of People	Number of Sites
Counterparts	26	24
Beneficiaries	22	24
Host family members	24	24
Stakeholders (Ministry officials)	4	
NGO staff	2	
Exchange program alumni	10	
Total	**88**	-

How Will the Information be Used?

The information gathered will inform Peace Corps staff at post and headquarters about host country nationals' perceptions of the community projects and the Volunteers. In conjunction with Volunteer feedback from the yearly Volunteer Survey and the Close-of-Service Surveys, this information will allow the Peace Corps to better understand its impact and address areas for improvement. For example, the information may be useful for Volunteer training and outreach to host families and project partners.

This information is also needed to provide performance information to the United States Office of Management and Budget and the United States Congress. As part of the Peace Corps Improvement Plan, drafted in response to its 2005 Program Assessment Rating Tool review, the Peace Corps proposed the creation of "baselines to measure results including survey data in countries with Peace Corps presence to measure the promotion of a better understanding of Americans on the part of the peoples served."[5] Feedback from the original pilots was used to revise the methodology rolled out to nine posts each in Fiscal Year 2009 and 2010, for a total of 18 posts across Peace Corps' three geographic regions: Africa; Inter-America and the Pacific; and Europe, Mediterranean and Asia. Taken together, these studies contribute to Peace Corps' ability to document the degree to which the agency is able to both meet the needs of host countries for trained men and women and to promote a better understanding of Americans among the peoples served.

---

[5] Downloaded from : http://www.whitehouse.gov/omb/expectmore/summary/10004615.2005.html 9-10-08

CHAPTER 2: PROJECT DESIGN AND PURPOSE

Sector Overview[6]

The pilot study evaluated the Peace Corps' Teaching English as a Foreign Language project in the education sector. The goal of the English Language Education Project is to assist Armenia in enhancing its participation in the international community by increasing the quality of English language programs and by providing new educational and community development opportunities throughout the country.

Initially, the English Language Education Project Volunteers were placed in the capital city of Yerevan. Over time, however, an increasing percentage of Volunteers were sent to small, rural towns and villages where the need for qualified English language teachers was greater. Major Armenian cities already had access to qualified English language instruction.

A model of the theory of change underlying the project approach is presented in Figure 1.

> **The English Language Education Project** helps improve the quality of English language education. The project also promotes youth civic engagement and service, including promoting the mobilization of youth and adults to meet the needs of their communities.

---

[6] The Sector Overview is based on the *English Language Education Project Plan* Dated January 2008.

Figure 1: Overview of the Theory of Change for the PC/Armenia English Language Education Project

Problem	Goals	Activities	Outcomes	Public Benefit
An insufficient number of: •Qualified English language teachers •High quality English language programs •Shortage of educational materials and resources	Goal 1: Improve students'/teachers' English language skills Goal 2: Improve teachers' English teaching practices Goal 3: Enhance English language curricula Goal 4: Expand English language opportunities between educational institutions and communities	Implementing new methods of classroom instruction, extra-curricular activities, and self-evaluation Skills transfer Promoting appropriate educational materials for schools and other local organizations Developing collaborations with target groups (e.g., NGOs)	Improved English competency among students and teachers Inclusion of interactive teaching strategies Greater civic involvement by students and teachers	Increased international involvement Higher quality education Increased community empowerment

This figure was compiled from information in the *Peace Corps/Armenia English Language Education Project: Project Plan.* January 2008.

English Language Education Project Volunteers develop English language skills by providing English language instruction in regular classroom settings, through English language clubs, and other extra-curricular activities Volunteers plan with their students. The activities are expected to promote personal and professional skills that enhance community development

The Volunteers address the needs of Armenian English language teachers through co-planning, team teaching, and by sponsoring teacher training workshops and conferences. Team-teaching was implemented in the English Language Education Project as a result of recommendations from the Inspector General's visit in November 2004. This change was designed to ensure that all Volunteers transfer knowledge and skills to Armenian teachers, that Volunteers were able to meet the professional standard of 15-20 hours of work per week within their primary assignment, and to promote a more productive relationship between Volunteers and counterparts.

In collaboration with Armenian teachers, Volunteers create appropriate educational materials and incorporate them into the English language curriculum. They also catalogue/organize the new materials in libraries and resource centers.

In accordance with the English Language Education Project Action Plan developed in 2007, Peace Corps Volunteers are placed at educational institutions, including secondary schools, colleges, universities, and the National Institute of Education.

CHAPTER 3: GOAL ONE FINDINGS

Performance under the Peace Corps' first goal was examined in two ways, by measuring:

1. The extent to which HCNs observed community and personal changes, reported gaining new technical skills, and the capacity to maintain the changes once the community project ended.

2. HCNs' satisfaction with the work of the community project, in particular, satisfaction with the extent to which their needs had been met.

Did the Peace Corps Projects Help Project Partners Meet Skill and Capacity Building Needs?

The English Language Education Project identified three outcomes related to skill and capacity building which Volunteers worked towards achieving with counterparts and beneficiaries:

1. Improved English language competency among students and teachers

2. Integration of interactive teaching strategies into classrooms

3. Greater civic involvement, particularly volunteerism, by students and teachers

The project goals focused on individual-level changes with regards to teaching practice and English language skills.

Findings on Individual Changes

This section starts with an overview of counterparts' prior professional experience. It continues with respondents' feedback about areas in which they changed information about how that change occurred, and the extent to which they have been able to maintain those changes after the departure of the Volunteer.

Prior Teaching and English Language Instruction Experience

The 26 counterparts (i.e., co-teachers) who worked with English Language Education Project Volunteers in Armenia already had significant experience with educational programs including English language programs (see Figure 2). All of the counterparts had worked as a teacher, master teacher, curriculum advisor, or school administrator for at least two years, with 76 percent of counterparts having worked in that field for more than 10 years.

Figure 2: Number of Years Counterparts (n=26) Have Worked in the Field

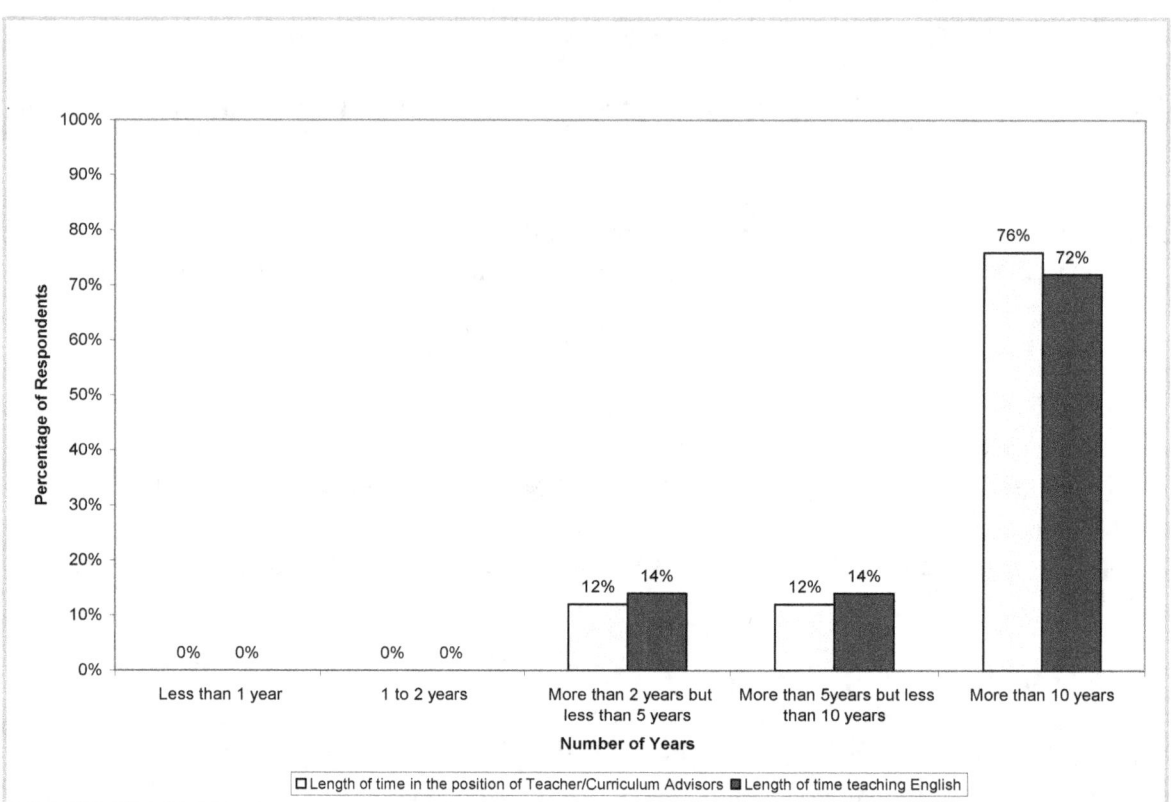

In What Ways Did Counterparts (Co-Teachers) and Beneficiaries (Students) Who Worked with Volunteers Change?

In the absence of data about conditions before the arrival of the Volunteers, counterparts and beneficiaries were asked to think back to *how they saw themselves* when they started working with a Volunteer and compare that to *how they currently see themselves.* They were then asked to report any changes they saw in themselves during that period. For each change mentioned, the counterparts and beneficiaries were asked whether they viewed the change as small, medium, or large, and the extent to which they attributed the changes to the interaction with the Volunteer.

Respondents reported a total of 194 changes. The range of skills acquired through the English Language Education Project can be categorized in five general areas:

1. Improved English language skills and different teaching methods (e.g., team teaching, new methods to teach critical thinking, lesson planning, the use of didactic materials)

2. New communication skills, teaching and using written and spoken English

3. More professionalism, but also less formality in approaches to treating students as individuals

4. Valuing different approaches and diversity among people, perceiving students differently, and volunteerism

5. New regard for their futures and the opportunities open to them

Forty-two percent of the changes referred to increases in specific skills (e.g., interactive teaching) or knowledge (e.g., English language) (Figure 3).

Figure 3: Ways Counterparts and Beneficiaries Changed Since the Start of the Peace Corps' Project (n= 194 changes)

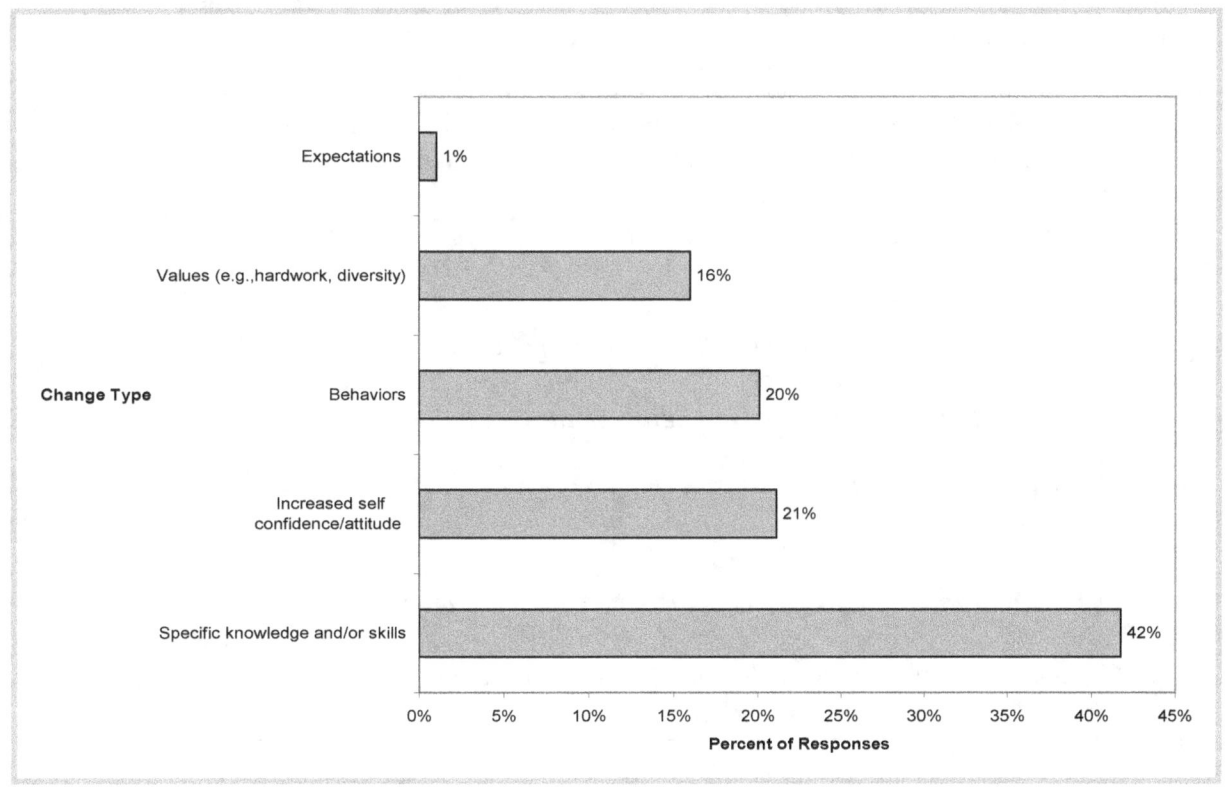

Students said they have learned to be more confident while speaking English, and in general they report that, due to their experience with a PCV, they are able to communicate with other English-speaking foreigners more freely and easily. Students also gained the skill and confidence to

search for and participate in various contests and programs, "Before I was afraid of failure. Now I realize that if you keep trying you will succeed."

Another student mentioned that due to a PCV's encouragement s/he succeeded in entering an exchange program. Many beneficiaries also mentioned skills gained in essay writing and computer operation. Some of the students participated in International Outreach Camps due to the assistance of a PCV. Three students mentioned that they organized classes for other young people, and one mentioned that the PCV inspired her/him to be willing to help others.

The two NGO counterparts described not only changes in personal characteristics, such as feeling more comfortable in expressing their opinions, but also saw improvements in practical skills related to time management, presentations, writing, appreciation of feedback, and conflict resolution.

While not a major theme in the students' responses, some mentioned that they were becoming more civic-minded. These students indicated that they were more aware of civic activities, but specific information about changes in their behaviors was not reported.

Counterparts and beneficiaries rated 85 percent of the changes as large and 85 percent were assessed as having been largely due to the Peace Corps' project. Counterparts and beneficiaries thought that 97 percent of the changes they noticed in themselves were maintained after the Volunteer left the community.

Examples of ways that counterparts (i.e., co-teachers) changed as a result of participation in the TEFL project

Professionalism (being on time, not talking on the phone at the lesson, planning).

I became more interested in the troubles of the community.

Now I don't avoid criticizing and being criticized.

Change in world outlook: I realize there is another mentality besides Armenian.

I keep an organizer now; it helps me with time management.

Creativity (changed way of thinking, attitude to the world and what we can do there. Before I wouldn't think of many solutions; now I see more).

Examples of ways that beneficiaries (i.e., students) changed as a result of participation in the TEFL project

For me these changes were critical, as I have changed my decision about my future profession.

I am personally very satisfied with changes. Now I can communicate with foreigners easily.

How Did Skills Transfer Occur?

The most useful thing that volunteers did was to facilitate open communication and interaction. Several respondents mentioned their ability to interact with a native English speaker and the "games" and other interactive methods that Volunteers used in their classrooms as the most helpful elements of the community projects. The participants in exchange programs not only mentioned open communication, but also mentioned the "value of getting a realistic picture of the United States from Volunteers" and "Volunteers' high level of effort and concern for the individuals and communities with which they worked."

Counterparts' comments about the most helpful aspects of the TEFL project

The unselfish approach to creating change and respect; organizing competitions, English groups, theatre plays, also presenting the American lifestyle and an alternative way of thinking.

Active communication was the most helpful for me. Also, it wasn't just speaking. We were conducting analytical work by examining translations of different authors. She [the Volunteer] began awarding certificates based on annual performance.

Another method for skills transfer through the English Language Education Project was the direct training of counterparts (i.e., co-teachers). In addition to the English language training that was part of the project, 52 percent of counterparts reported receiving counterpart training and 42 percent received Project Design and Management (PDM) training (Figure 4). Those who received training said the courses were useful.

Figure 4: Counterpart Training (n=26)

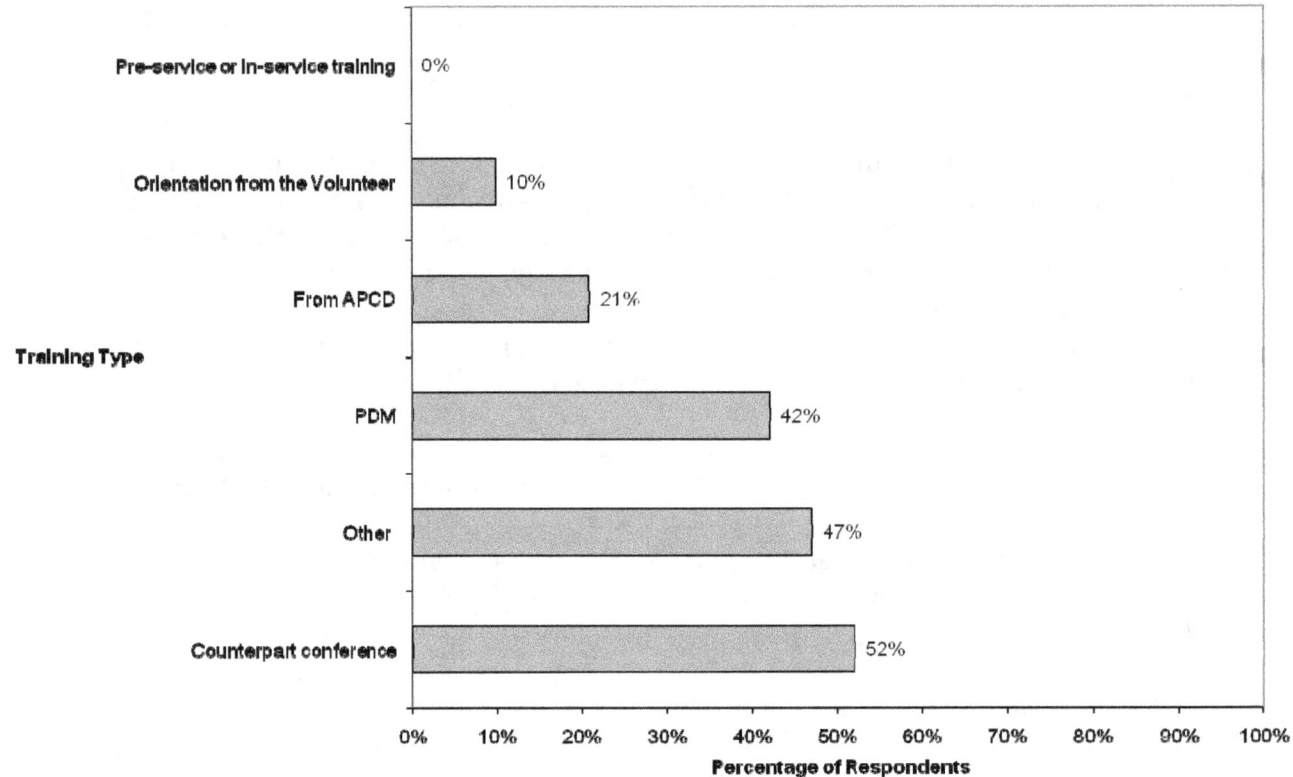

Counterparts' comments about training usefulness

We got acquainted with their [Volunteers'] approaches. They are very goal-seeking and purposeful and enthusiastic in any initiative. Their excitement about the approach was contagious.

APCD and counterpart conferences were interesting for me in terms of the exchange with other counterparts. The experience made me realize that my previous PCVs had done a good job. PDM training was quite useful.

Organizational Change

This section discusses changes at the school and community levels that occurred as a result of the Peace Corps project.

In What Ways Did Schools and Other Partner Organizations Change?

In the absence of data about conditions before the arrival of the Volunteers, counterparts and beneficiaries were asked to think back to how *they saw school and its English language program*, and/or the larger community, when the Volunteer arrived and compare that to how *they currently see the program and/or community*. They were asked to report any changes in the school, in its English language program and in the larger community during that period. For each change mentioned, the counterparts and beneficiaries were asked whether they viewed the change as small, medium, or large, and the extent to which they attributed the changes to the interaction with the Volunteer.

Over 190 changes were reported.

Sixty-two percent of the counterparts, beneficiaries, NGO staff, and exchange alumni said that their English language programs were better as a result of the English Language Education Project. Eighty-eight percent of respondents said that English language opportunities, such as English language clubs, were at least somewhat better. Forty-five percent of the changes mentioned referred to changes in teaching methods that had been adopted in the classroom. Many respondents described other changes introduced into the school, such as using a wider range of educational materials during lessons, setting up an English laboratory, and changes in teaching approaches The latter included a more open and creative teaching style that demonstrated greater respect for students than was the norm (including treating them as individuals). Other changes included improved English language skills among teachers and improved teaching/classroom management methods, as well as increased knowledge about the United States (Figure 5).

Figure 5: Ways Schools and/or Communities Changed from the Start of the Peace Corps' Project (n=190 changes)

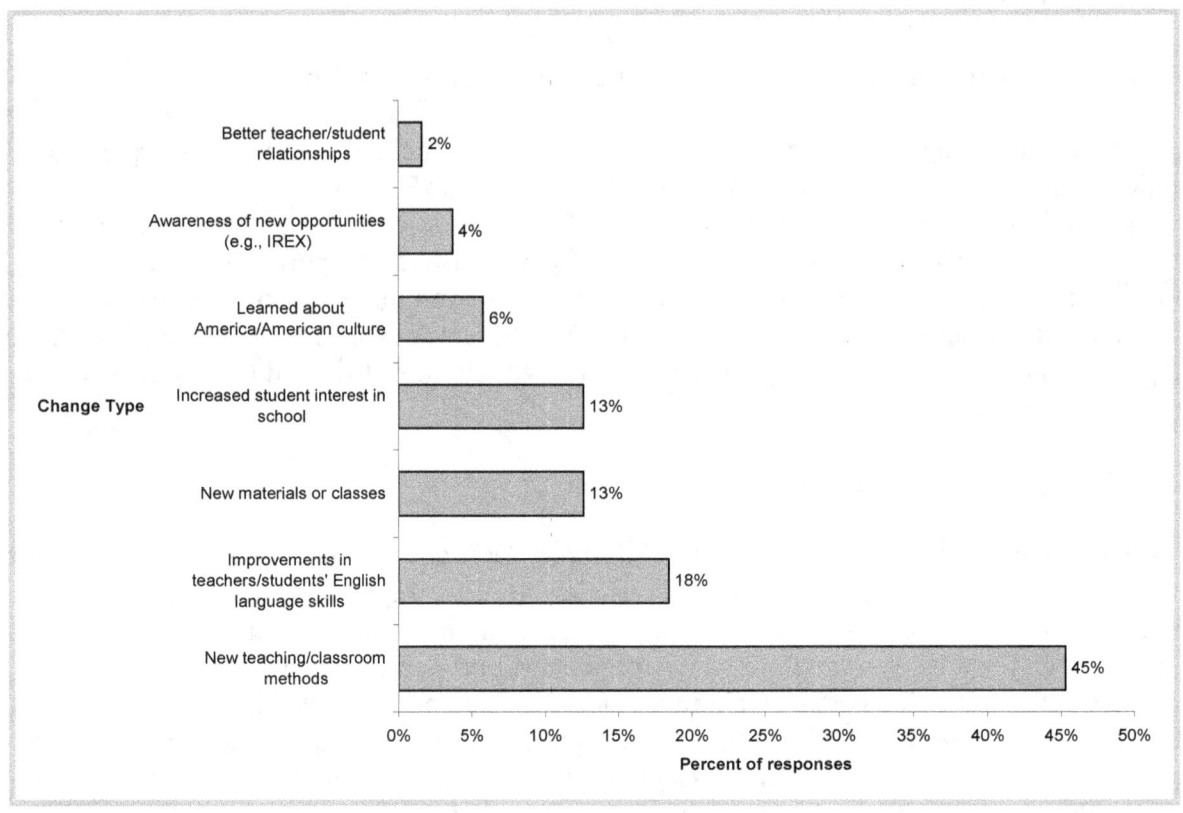

In sites that no longer had a serving Volunteer, counterparts and beneficiaries indicated that 74 percent of the changes had been maintained.

New teaching methods reported as a result of the TEFL program

[A] *transition from an academic style of teaching to a more practical and interactive style.*

Students' attitudes toward learning have changed; they gained self-motivation and learned the concept of democratic decision-making.

For those students who do not have opportunity to study English, (e.g. those studying German), or who want to perfect their English, the English Club is a very good opportunity.

Did skills transfer lead to sustainable organizational change?

Sixty-two percent of counterparts reported that the Volunteers' work in schools was, or could be, maintained to a large extent and 80 percent reported that the work in the community was, or could be, maintained to a small extent (see Figure 6).

Figure 6: Extent to Which Volunteer's work was Sustained After Volunteer Departure: Armenia

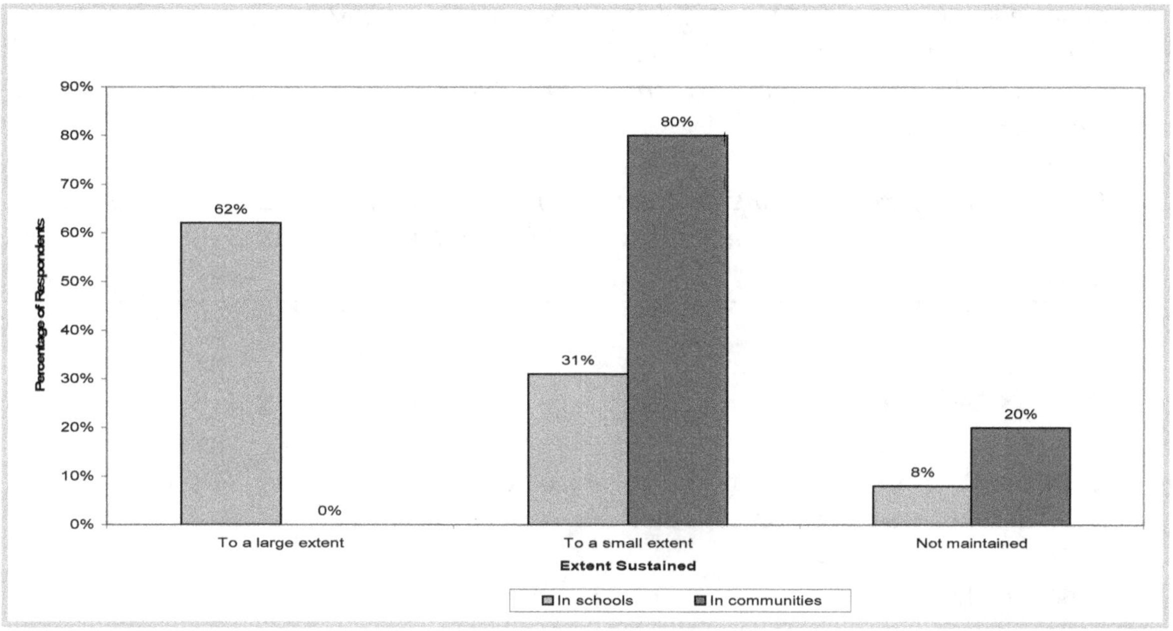

Counterparts' (i.e., co-teachers') views of the long- term impact of the project

The English language will be more accessible to everyone, and people will be more familiar with U.S. culture.

Materials left will be a very useful tool for further studies and development.

I don't think it will have a lasting effect. It will affect only the teachers and students [the Volunteer] communicated and worked with. Other teachers are not interested and enthusiastic to communicate and teach with him, maybe it's a function of their age.

Beneficiaries' (i.e., students) views of project impact

All this is useful and applicable to my every-day life. I use presentation skills and team work while studying at the university. The time management and scheduling is also quite useful.

The most valuable thing that I gained was the idea of volunteer work.

I continue participating in contests, and [the Volunteer] had taught me to do that. I used my English in communicating with the U.S. Embassy representative when in Camp (Camp GLOW), and I use English when speaking with other PCVs.

I changed my mind regarding my future profession: I didn't love English at all, and wanted to be a doctor, but now I want to be an English language specialist.

Overall HCN Satisfaction

Three measures of overall satisfaction with the Peace Corps' project were included in the interviews. These were satisfaction with the:

- Reported changes
- Collaboration with Peace Corps Volunteers
- Degree to which the project met their needs

The findings on these questions are reported below.

Eighty-four percent of counterparts (i.e., co- teachers), were at least somewhat satisfied with the changes in the schools and 73 percent with changes in their communities. Ninety-six percent of beneficiaries (i.e., students) were at least somewhat satisfied with the changes in their schools (Figure 7).

Students not only noted changes in teaching methods and increased interest in English, but also the more general influence that PCVs had on students—helping them to think independently and feel more confident. At the same time, concern about the issue of sustainability was mentioned by students as well: "When she was here it was okay, but when she left everything went back to the same," and "The results are not so evident, the quality of teaching hasn't changed."

The respondents from stakeholder agencies expressed the opinion that even though there is still more to do, the changes realized through the Peace Corps project are significant for developing school capacities.

Figure 7: Satisfaction with Organizational/Community Changes as a Result of the Peace Corps' Projects Counterpart (n=26) and Beneficiary (n=22)

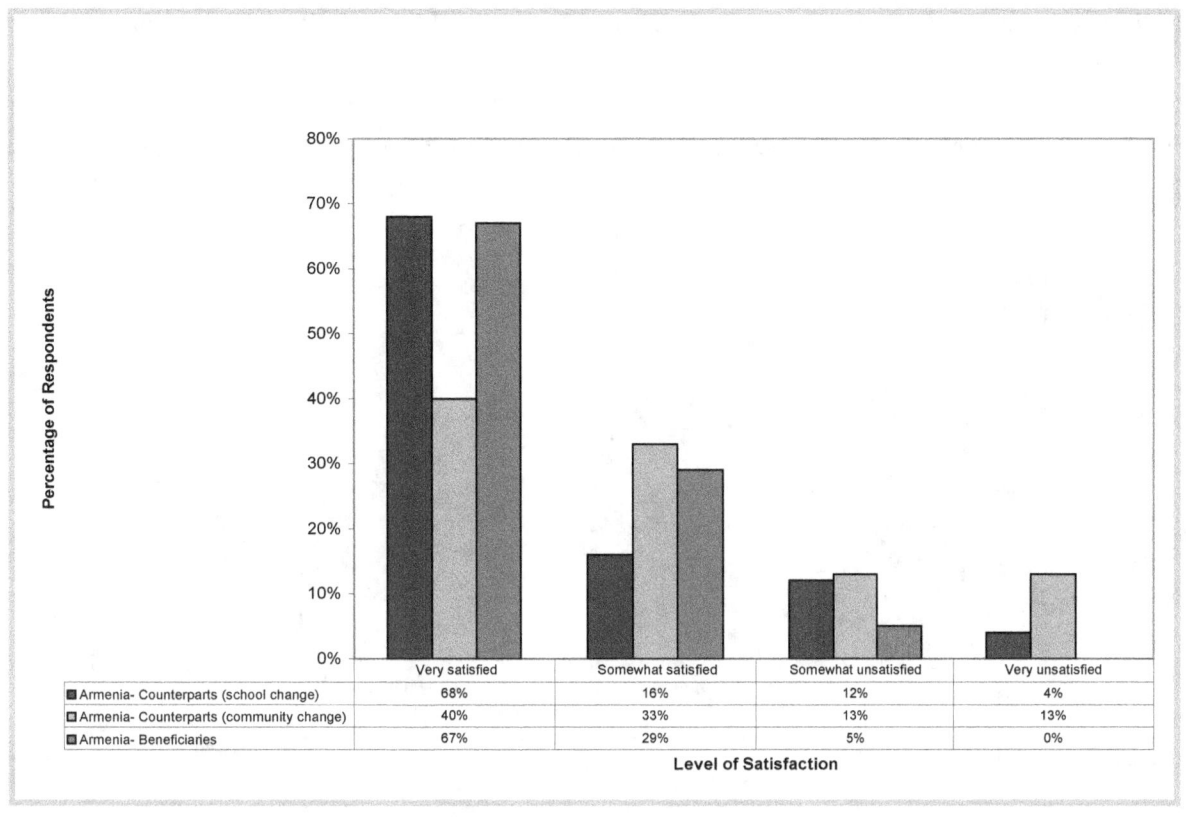

	Very satisfied	Somewhat satisfied	Somewhat unsatisfied	Very unsatisfied
■ Armenia- Counterparts (school change)	68%	16%	12%	4%
▨ Armenia- Counterparts (community change)	40%	33%	13%	13%
■ Armenia- Beneficiaries	67%	29%	5%	0%

Findings on Collaboration with the Peace Corps

Ninety-two percent of counterparts and three out of the four stakeholders (i.e., ministry officials) interviewed reported that they were satisfied or very satisfied with the level of collaboration between their schools and the Peace Corps (Figure 8).

Figure 8: Satisfaction with Level of Collaboration: Counterpart (n=26) and Stakeholder (n=4)[7]

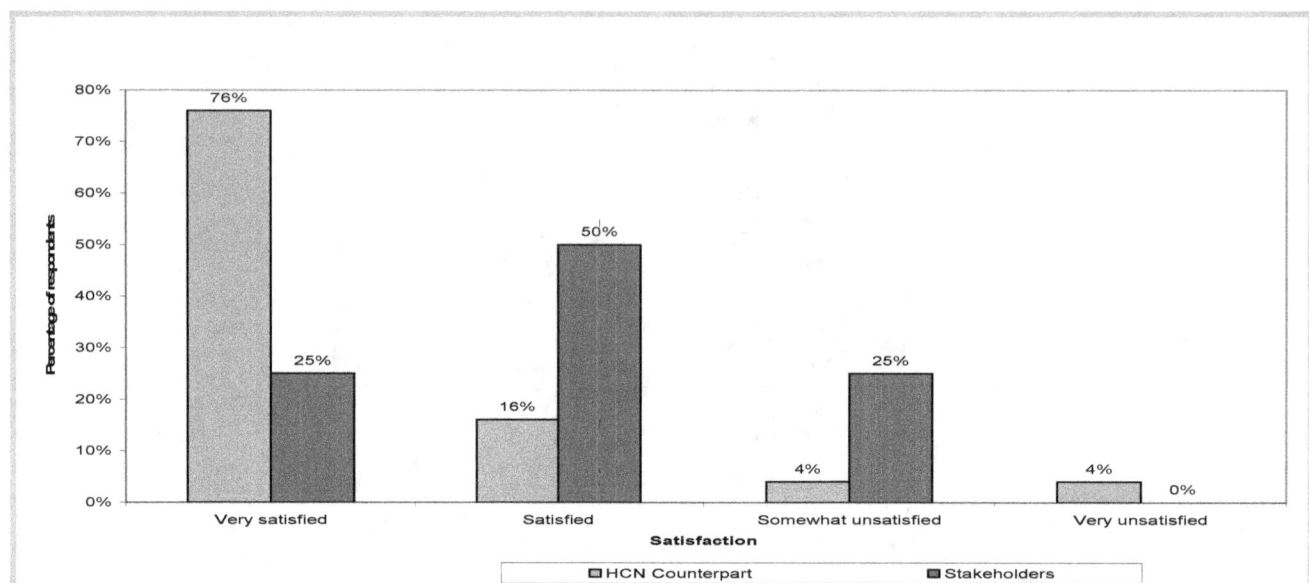

Counterparts' descriptions of collaboration

The collaboration was very productive; all the teachers were trying to speak English. The PCV was also helping other teachers.

Very satisfied, especially with respect to joint work among the teachers and the introduction of collaborative methods of teaching.

---

[7] Collaboration refers to the level of partnership and joint work on Peace Corps projects

Did HCN Think that Their Needs Were Met

Eighty-two percent of counterparts indicated that the Peace Corps' projects met their school's needs. Both of the NGO staff members who responded said that the project met their organization's needs completely or to a large extent. A lack of technical equipment and didactic materials were the main unmet needs. Respondents were less knowledgeable about the degree to which community needs had been met. Forty-two percent of respondents did not know whether community needs were met and only 35 percent said that needs were met completely or to a large extent (see Figure 9).

Figure 9: Extent to Which the English Language Education Project Met Counterparts (n=26) and NGO staff Needs (n=4)

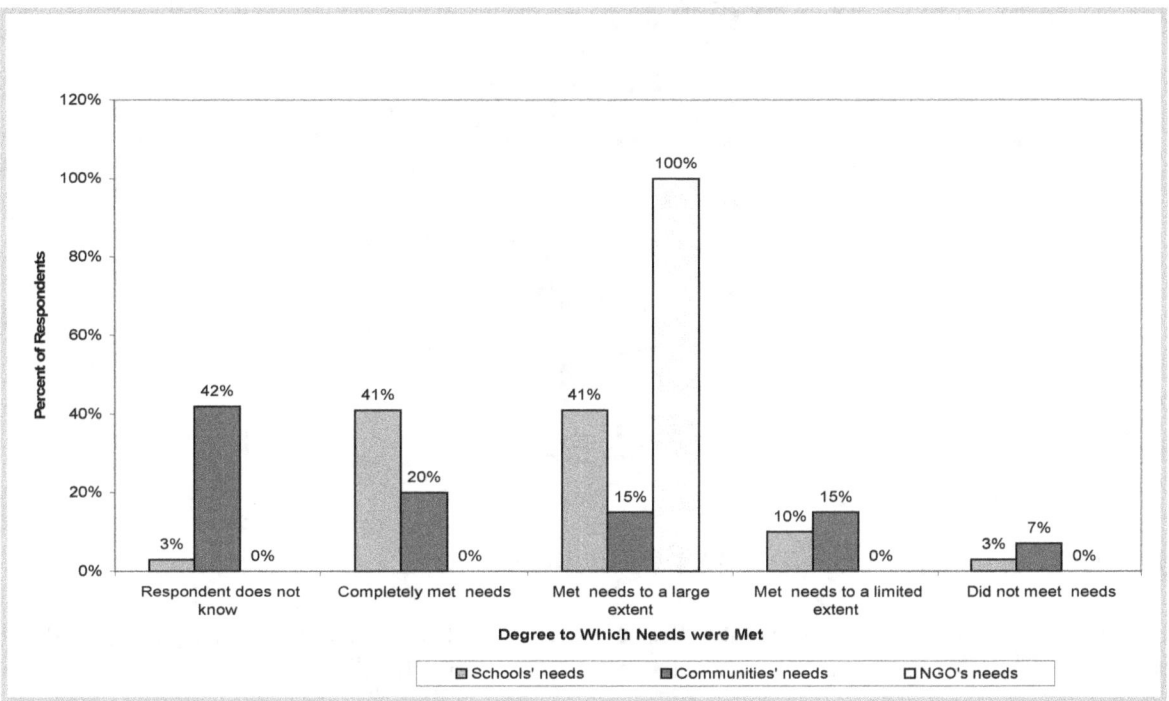

Would HCNs Want to Work with the Peace Corps Again?

Another measure of satisfaction with the Peace Corps is counterpart's desire to work with another Volunteer. Eighty-one percent of counterparts reported that they would welcome another Volunteer, eighteen percent were unsure, and two percent said that they would not want another Volunteer. Respondents who said that they were unsure whether they would want another Volunteer noted that in some cases they did not see a real value in having a Volunteer and in other cases they would want another Volunteer only if that person were well-trained and hard-working.

Ninety-seven percent of counterparts reported that as a result of their experiences, their opinion of the Peace Corps was positive (see Figure 10).

Figure 10: Counterparts' Overall Opinion of Peace Corps/Armenia (n=26)

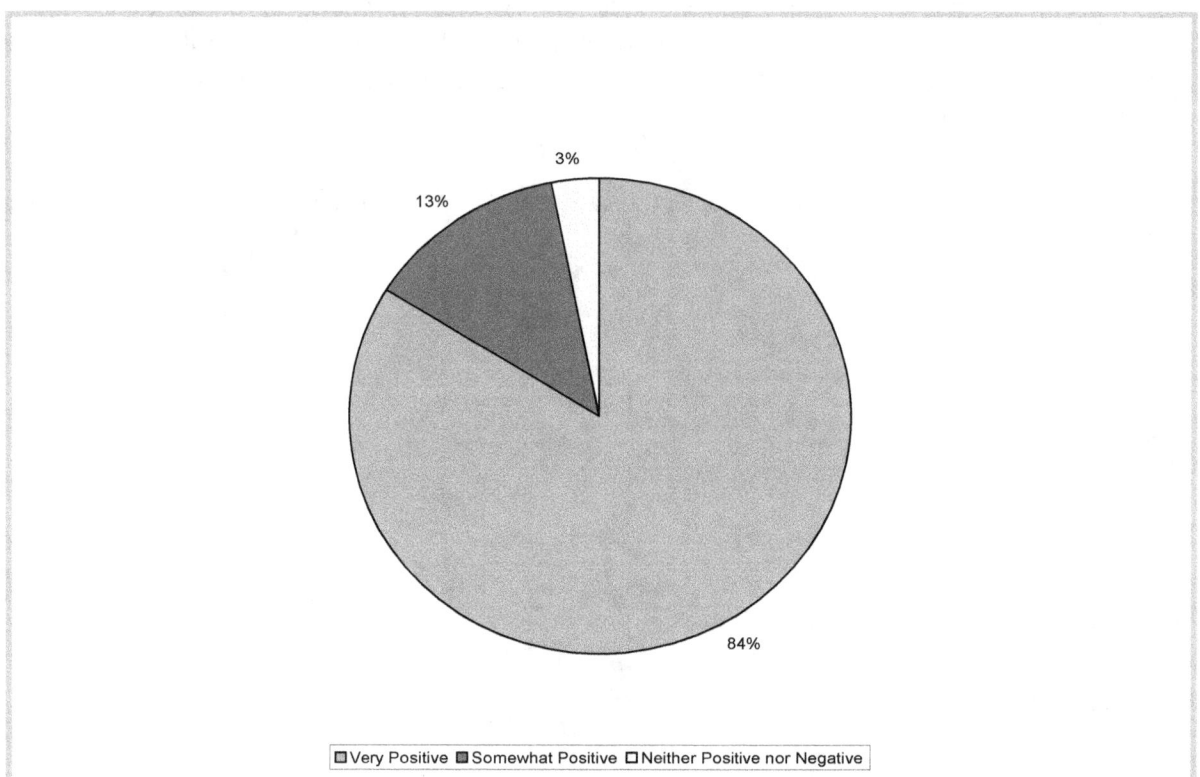

Support and Barriers to Project Performance

When asked about advice for other sites that planned to implement a similar project, counterparts commented that schools should be ready to collaborate, work hard, and be flexible.

The main factors contributing to project success, reported by beneficiaries and counterparts, were:

1. Teamwork and coordination

2. Perseverance of school staff and Volunteers

3. Having access to a native English speaker

4. Support from the school administration

Counterpart comment about the most helpful aspect of the project

He was a real pedagogue, he related to students in the right way. He could teach us very professionally. But, the most useful thing was communication with a native speaker.

Barriers to project success included the limited class time available and cultural differences. Limited class time was cited as a reason that English language skills and teaching methods did not improve more. Cultural differences were typically used to refer to PCVs who were less hierarchical in their interactions with students and did not use some of the more severe disciplinary methods common in Armenian classrooms. These differences produced a lack of respect for the PCV among students and teachers. In a few cases, lack of support from the school administration was mentioned as a barrier to success. One counterpart specifically suggested that the project explore a way to add a financial benefit for participating schools in order to encourage teachers and administrative staff to more strongly support the work of the PCV and to maintain the changes once the PCV had departed.

Counterparts' perceptions of barriers to program success

Some misunderstanding related to the different cultures. PCV's hot temper and some untidiness.

Director of the school is not supportive at all. Very often [he]is not in his office and cannot be reached. [He] does not care about the project at all.

Our guys mock some of the male PCVs. Also, I know that local authorities do not support them in their initiatives. The director didn't support them in the creation of computer lab.

Areas for further research

Based on the responses collected, four main themes emerged for further investigation:

1. Pre-implementation preparation

2. Planning for sustainability

3. Amount of time dedicated to English language programming/teaching

4. Stakeholder involvement

Respondents' comments related to each theme are provided below. The post may want to explore these issues both to determine the extent of any problems and, where needed, to develop ways to address the issues raised.

Pre-Implementation Preparation: Only 28 percent of counterparts reported that they had either a somewhat or very clear understanding of what the project would do before it began (see Figure 11).

Figure 11: Counterparts' Opinion of Pre-implementation Project Clarity: Armenia (n=26)

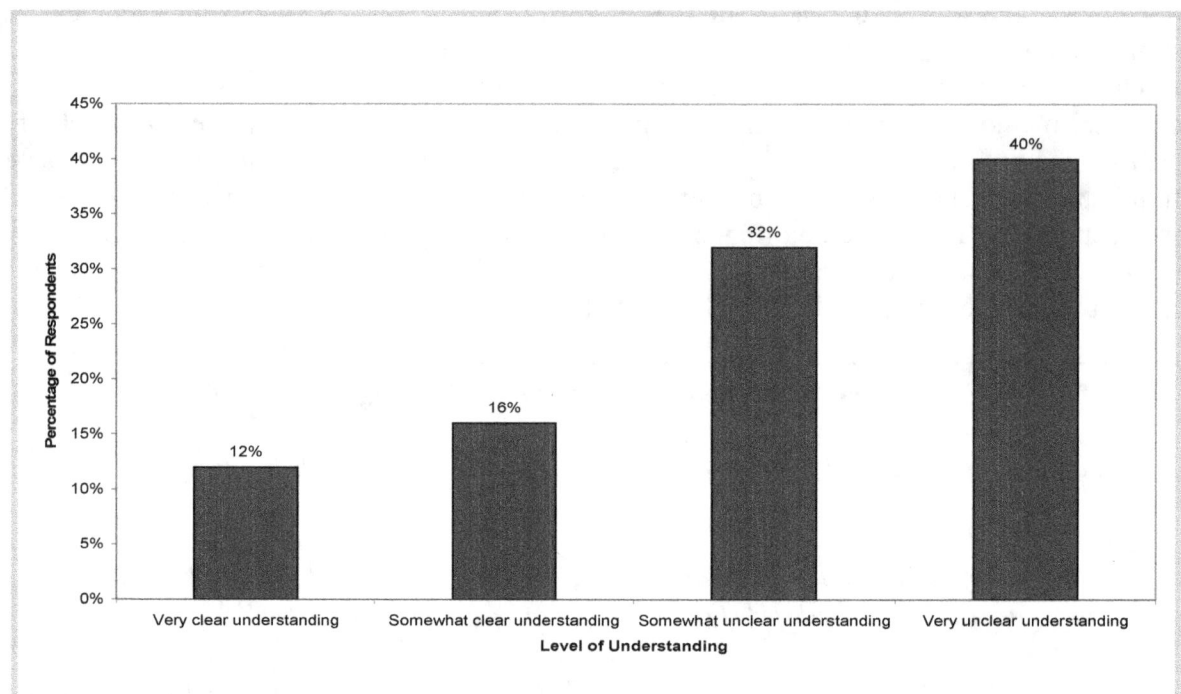

When asked about the basis for their understanding, counterparts mentioned that they were relying on their experiences with prior Volunteers. When they were asked what schools should do to prepare for Volunteers, developing and communicating a clear purpose for the project was the main solution proposed.

Counterparts' comments about pre-implementation preparation

Based on my previous experience with PCVs from the YMCA, I knew that I shouldn't have too high level of expectation. I realized that the counterpart should support and direct him instead of waiting for the PCV to do something.

We didn't have a clear understanding, but were very optimistic about this opportunity

---

Planning for sustainability: The most frequently cited reason to explain why it was hard to maintain the project was a lack of leadership support (35 percent), and for one NGO staff member, it was a lack of skilled staff (Figure 12).

Figure 12: Factors that Impeded Sustainability of Project Changes: Armenia

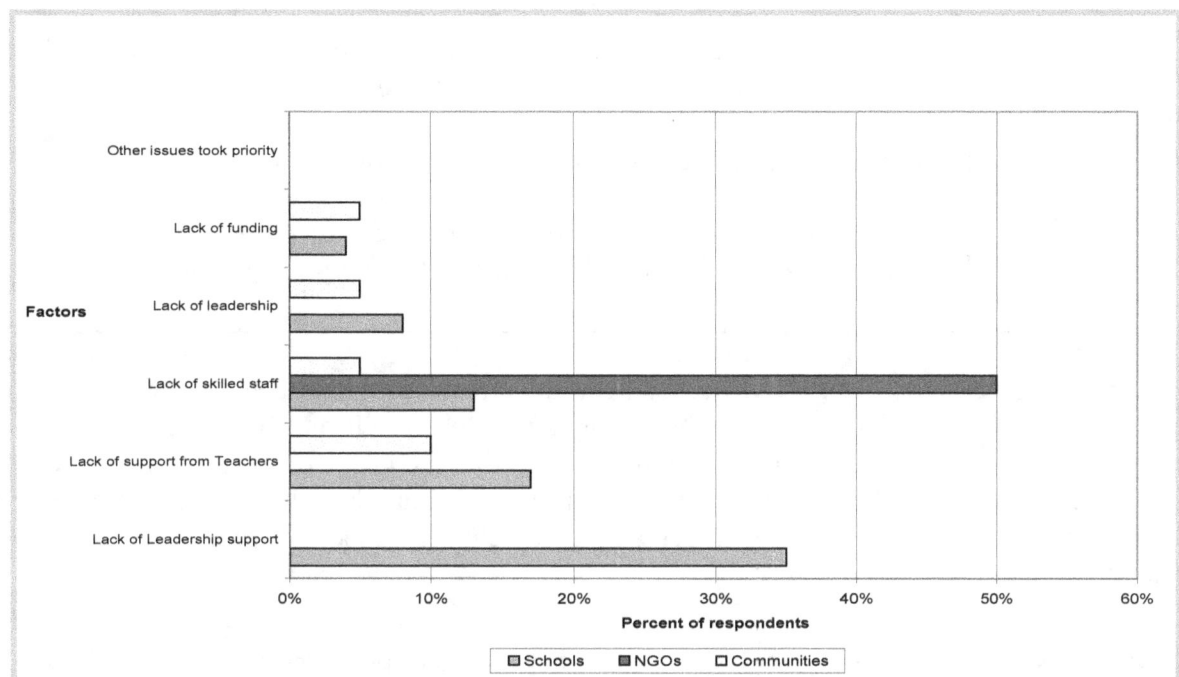

The Armenian research team commented that there were structural barriers to project sustainability. "In some sites, there were circumstances that made the PCV's work difficult, (e.g., school administration or harsh competition between schools that made their collaboration limited.)" Three PCVs mentioned that since the English language program had been approved by the Government of Armenia, it was difficult to modify the program. One PCV said, "There is an emerging need to change the national English teaching program and the textbooks, but a PCV does not have any influence at that level."

Some of the counterparts also mentioned conflict between the Government's English language program and the new methods and approaches brought by Volunteers. "All this is good after classes, but not during the classes," one PCV said. "My counterpart says the Government of Armenia program is too rich and complicated and informative; thus they do not have time 'to play games' (interactive teaching methods) during lessons" (CDPF, page 22).

Amount of time dedicated to English language programming/teaching: When asked what they would change about the project, both counterparts and beneficiaries mentioned the inadequate amount of time available for learning. Respondents said that they wanted longer and more frequent sessions and club meetings. Counterparts also commented that they would like to have continuous Volunteer support over successive years.

Regarding the change in teaching methods, the respondents stated that the teaching program is set by the government and could not be significantly changed, thus hindering the impact of PCVs.

Counterpart's comment regarding the long-term effects of Volunteers

They lay a good foundation for English language teaching; now we need PCVs each year in order for it to become effective. [A] two year break is undesirable.

Stakeholder's comment regarding the long-term effects of Volunteers

I think the Peace Corps should consider all the experience gained and propose changes to the English program in secondary schools to the Ministry. That could cause a change in policy level.

Stakeholder involvement: The four project stakeholders interviewed indicated limited awareness of specific initiatives of the English Language Education Project (see Figure 13). When asked how they promote the projects and activities that the Peace Corps has within the schools, three of the four stakeholders mentioned that they continually talk about the value of the English Language Education Project. The remaining stakeholder responded that he did not promote the project.

Figure 13: Stakeholder Awareness (n=4) of In-Country Peace Corps Activities: Armenia

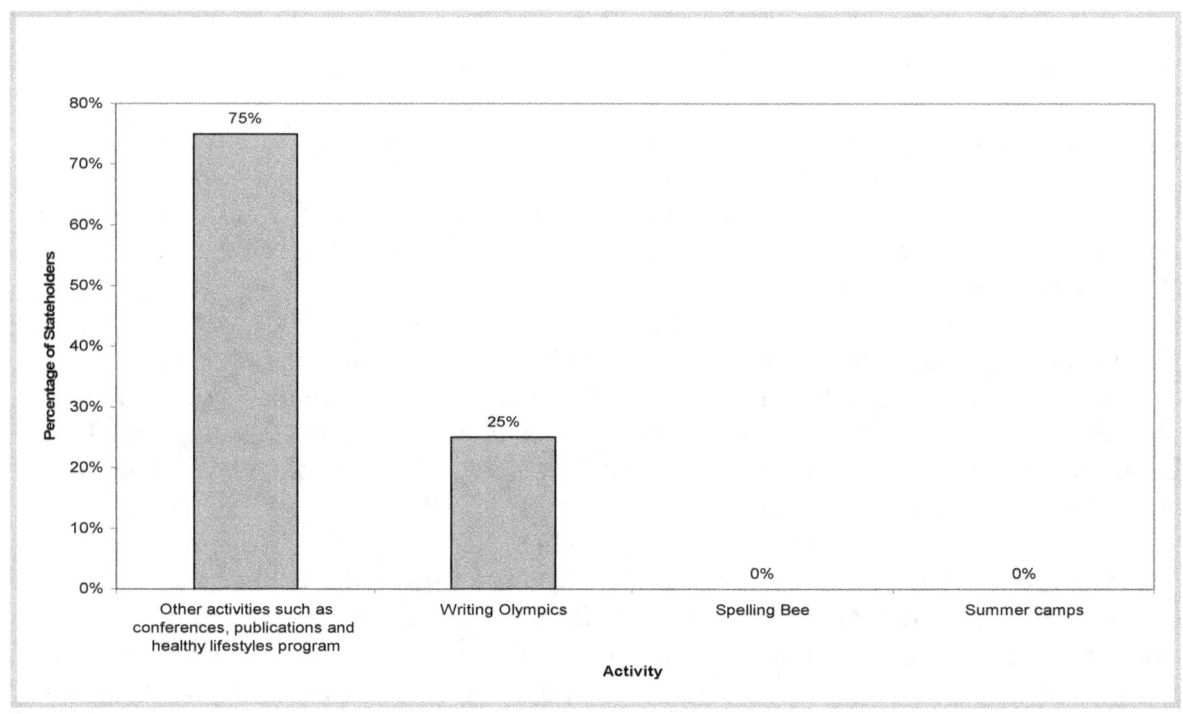

CHAPTER 4: GOAL TWO FINDINGS

This section addresses how and to what extent Volunteers promoted a better understanding of Americans among the HCNs with whom they lived and worked. The section begins with a description of what Armenians thought about Americans prior to working with a Volunteer and how they acquired that information. The section continues with a description of how much and in what ways Armenians interacted with Volunteers and concludes with their opinions of Americans after interacting with Volunteers.

How Did Armenians Obtain Information about Americans Prior to Interacting with a Volunteer?

All HCNs, excluding ministry officials, were asked if they had received information about Americans prior to interacting with the Volunteers. All but one of the 84 respondents reported that they had some prior knowledge of Americans.

The most frequently mentioned sources of information were television and movies, with 67 percent of the counterparts and host family members mentioning those as sources (Figure 14). Sixty-three percent of counterparts, beneficiaries, NGO staff, and exchange alumni mentioned schools as the second most frequent source of information. Conversations among friends and family were the second most frequently mentioned source by 54 percent of host family members. Eighteen percent of counterparts mentioned the Internet as a source of information about Americans.

Figure 14: Source of Information about Americans Prior to Interacting with a Volunteer: Armenia

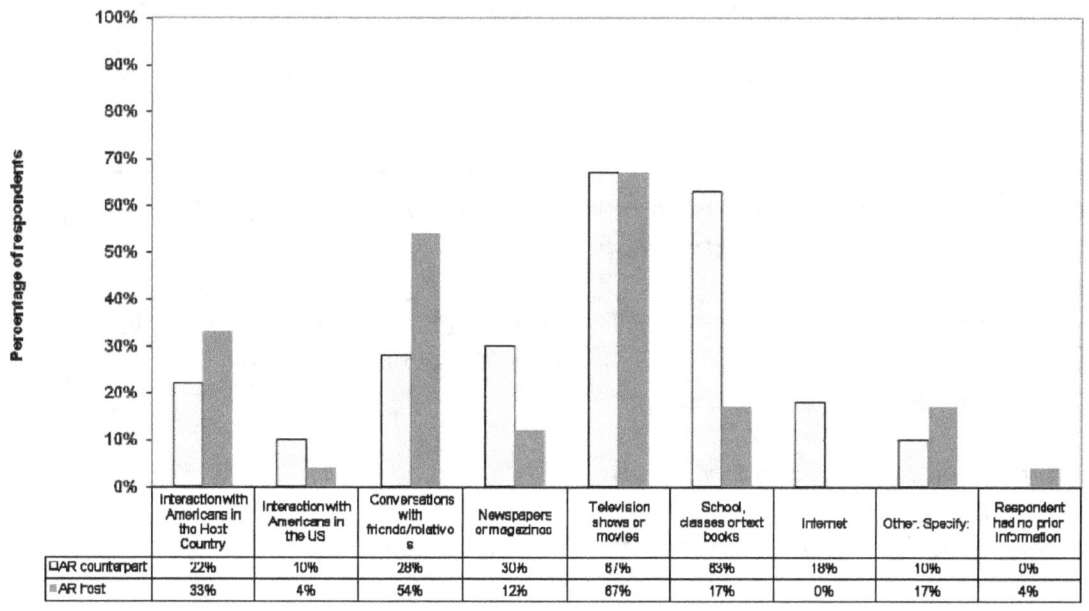

	Interaction with Americans in the Host Country	Interaction with Americans in the US	Conversations with friends/relatives	Newspapers or magazines	Television shows or movies	School, classes or text books	Internet	Other: Specify:	Respondent had no prior information
AR counterpart	22%	10%	28%	30%	67%	63%	18%	10%	0%
AR host	33%	4%	54%	12%	67%	17%	0%	17%	4%

What Were Respondents' Opinions About Americans Prior to Interacting with the Volunteer?

Many respondents reported negative views of Americans when asked for their opinions of Americans prior to interacting with a Volunteer. Counterparts and beneficiaries both reported prior opinions of Americans as "cold" (6 responses), hard-hearted (3), reserved (6), unsociable (3), unfriendly (6), aggressive (3), and unscrupulous." NGO staff and exchange alumni reported these same opinions, as well as concerns about whether they would be able to work with Americans.

Counterparts' opinions about Americans prior to interacting with a Volunteer

I thought of them as lacking human characteristics and conscience, which later was changed. I thought they were indifferent towards other people.

Cold, not friendly, selfish, conqueror, with artificial smile, spy, not hospitable.

I imagine them as an a isolated, reserved, closed people. "Unbookish" and not having comprehensive knowledge, with narrow specialization. Also, I thought of them as untidy persons.

Students, especially those from rural communities, often described Americans in terms of their physical appearance. Their most typical perception of an American before getting to know Volunteers was a "thin man or woman with blond hair that had an artificial smile." Some students mentioned, "I imagine men are tall, muscular, and brutal"; "I thought everyone there is beautiful." In two cases out of five, the students imagined an African American as a typical representative of the United States.

Beneficiaries' opinions about Americans prior to interacting with a Volunteer

I don't remember exactly my previous perception of Americans, but I did not have a good opinion of them because I didn't like America. I thought of them as unconcerned people, laughing all the time.

Cold, dispassionate, unsociable, a cool card.

Easy manners, not limiting their wishes, informal in their dress, different from Russians.

They are very open-minded, too liberal, egotistical and ill-mannered.

NGO staff's and exchange alumni's opinions about Americans prior to interacting with this Volunteer

NGO staff:

> *The perception was quite negative. The Soviet ideology created an image of a hostile, aggressive, and war-like country.*

Exchange alumni:

> *I think of them as people who are reserved and indifferent toward others. I thought they did not appreciate friendship and family much. They did not have high moral standards and values. I thought they were hard workers, who did not spend much time on relationships.*
>
> *I thought of them as aggressive, stupid, narrow-minded, slovenly people who use profane language.*

Host family members also reported negative prior opinions, but they focused somewhat more on lifestyle issues, such as being unclean and unfriendly, than on Volunteers' work ethic.

Among all respondents, when positive prior opinions were described, they focused on Americans being hard working and care-free.

Host family members' opinions about Americans prior to interacting with this Volunteer:

> *I thought of them as indifferent and slovenly people. I had a negative perception about them as immoral and depraved people.*
>
> *I thought they are specialized in a certain narrow field, like robots. I imagine them as a hard-hearted people.*
>
> *Not interacting, unfriendly, because they are a collection and not a nation, egocentric.*
>
> *They like to interact, but they are not friendly. They are kind, accurate, and stingy.*

To What Extent Did HCNs Have Experience with the Peace Corps and Volunteers?

All respondents were asked if they had known more than one Volunteer. In Armenia, many Peace Corps partners had known several Volunteers. Counterparts (i.e., co-teachers) and beneficiaries (i.e., students) reported knowing two or three Volunteers, while NGO staff reported having known an average of six Volunteers. Exchange program alumni reported knowing an average of five Volunteers. Counterparts and exchange program alumni reported working with Volunteers for an average of 29 months; beneficiaries reported working with Volunteers for an average of 24 months. Both of the NGO staff had worked with Volunteers for at least two years.

Host family members reported that, on average, the number of Volunteers hosted was two and the average length of stay was eight months.

How Much and What Kinds of Contact Did HCNs Have with Volunteers?

Goal 2 of the Peace Corps is rooted in the belief that through frequent and varied interaction with Volunteers, HCNs will better understand Americans. This section describes the number and types of interactions that HCNs had with Volunteers.

Host Family Members: When asked about the types of things that respondents did with the Volunteers that they hosted, all of the 24 host family members interviewed indicated that they ate meals together, and at least 75 percent responded that they socialized together, ran errands together, and talked about each others' friends/families and lives (Figure 15).

Figure 15: Activities that Host Family Members and Volunteers Shared: Armenia (n=24)

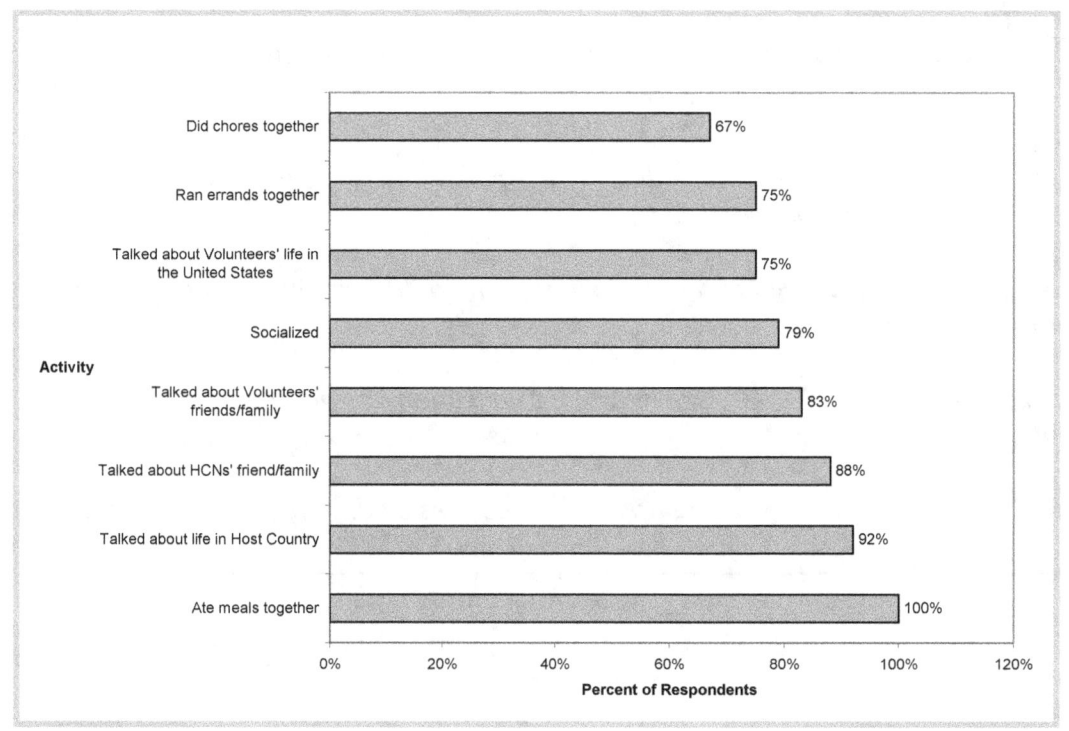

Eighty-three percent of host family members rated their relationships with the Volunteers they hosted as positive in nature. Forty-five percent reported that they were very close and thought of the Volunteer as family. However, 17 percent of host family members rated their relationships with the Volunteers they hosted as not very close at all (see Figure 16).

Figure 16: Host Family Rating of Their Relationship with the Volunteer: Armenia (n=24)

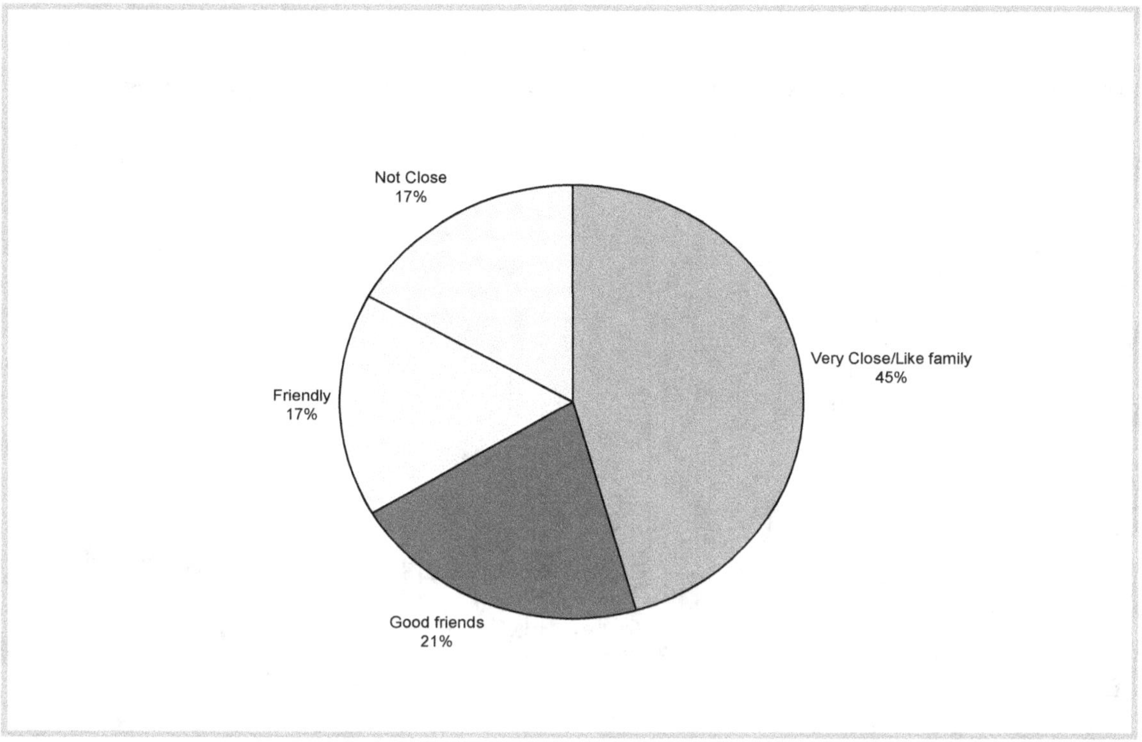

Host family members' opinions of the hosting experience:

He was like a member of our family. When he was leaving and packed things it was very difficult to part with him. We become involved with him and we were feeling his absence for a long time.

She was a very good person, even wrote a thank-you letter in Armenian for us when leaving. She helped me in making preserves, her parents visited her and we were happy to host them, we took her to all parties we attended.

He wouldn't interact, was very sloppy, didn't clean his room, didn't wash dishes after himself, and wore the same clothes. He would hardly participate at gatherings and sometimes didn't exchange a word with us.

They were educated and interesting people, but our interests were different. He never bought anything for the home to treat together. He was a very stingy man. He was never doing the things mentioned in the contract - his obligations.

Host country counterparts, beneficiaries, NGO staff, and exchange alumni: Responses varied in terms of how often counterparts, beneficiaries, NGO staff, and exchange alumni interacted with Volunteers. Beneficiaries and counterparts reported seeing Volunteers either daily or several times a week. Exchange alumni reported seeing Volunteers weekly or monthly. NGO staff split, with one of the two respondents saying that he saw the Volunteer several times a week and the other saying that he saw the Volunteer weekly. Although few respondents saw Volunteers socially on a daily basis, many saw them at least weekly in a social setting (Figure 17).

Figure 17: Frequency of Volunteer Interaction with Counterparts and Beneficiaries: Armenia

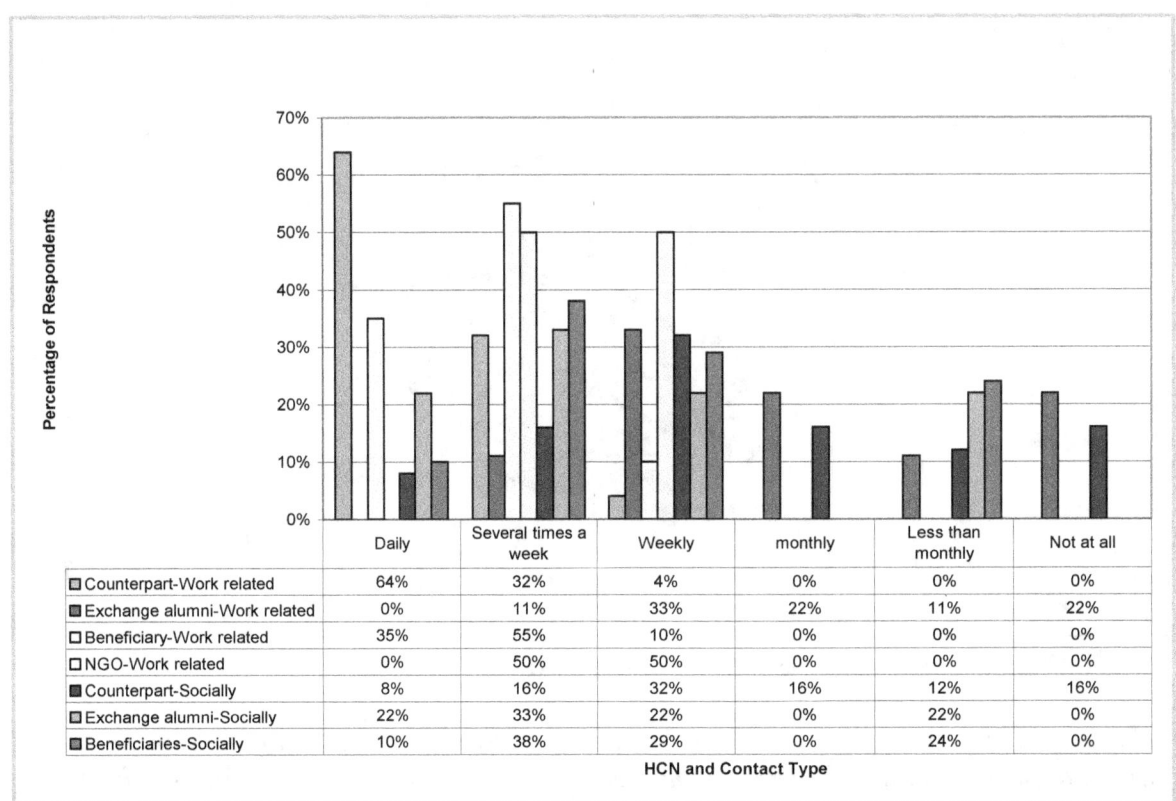

	Daily	Several times a week	Weekly	monthly	Less than monthly	Not at all
☐ Counterpart-Work related	64%	32%	4%	0%	0%	0%
■ Exchange alumni-Work related	0%	11%	33%	22%	11%	22%
☐ Beneficiary-Work related	35%	55%	10%	0%	0%	0%
☐ NGO-Work related	0%	50%	50%	0%	0%	0%
■ Counterpart-Socially	8%	16%	32%	16%	12%	16%
☐ Exchange alumni-Socially	22%	33%	22%	0%	22%	0%
■ Beneficiaries-Socially	10%	38%	29%	0%	24%	0%

HCN and Contact Type

Changes in HCN's Understanding of Americans After Knowing Volunteers

This section provides information about changes in HCNs' opinions of Americans as well as some detail about the types of things they learned about Americans from interacting with Volunteers.

Were Respondents' Opinions of Americans Better or Worse After Interacting with a Volunteer?

After the Peace Corps experience, 71 percent of counterparts, 72 percent of beneficiaries, and 100 percent of the 10 exchange alumni had more positive views of Americans. Among NGO staff and ministry officials, half reported more positive views and half reported that their views had not changed. Among host family members, 52 percent reported more positive views and 14 percent reported less positive views of Americans after living with Volunteers (see Figure 18).

Figure 18: Host Country Nationals' Change in Opinion of Americans after Contact with Volunteers: Armenia

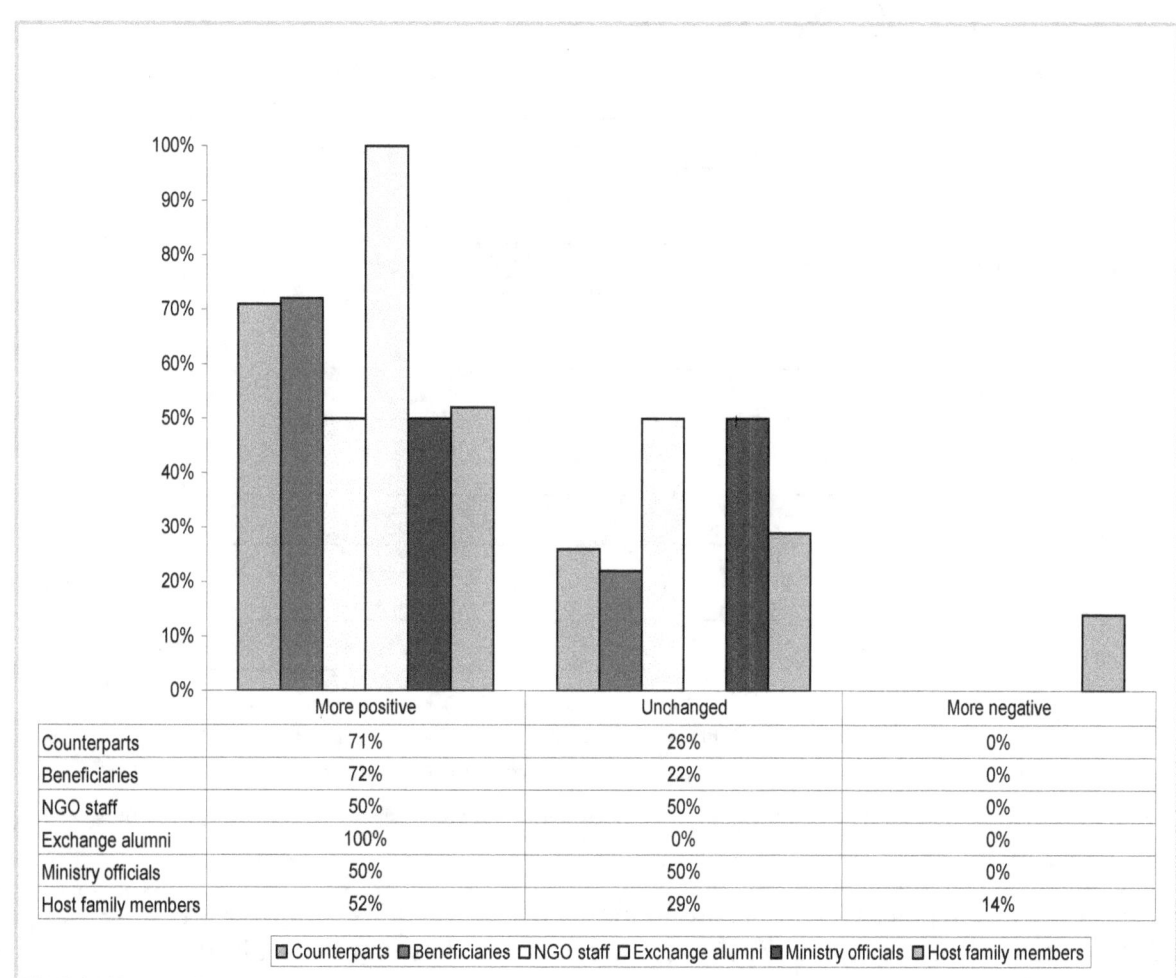

	More positive	Unchanged	More negative
Counterparts	71%	26%	0%
Beneficiaries	72%	22%	0%
NGO staff	50%	50%	0%
Exchange alumni	100%	0%	0%
Ministry officials	50%	50%	0%
Host family members	52%	29%	14%

□ Counterparts ■ Beneficiaries □ NGO staff □ Exchange alumni ■ Ministry officials □ Host family members

Findings on What Armenians Learned About Americans from Volunteers

When host family members were asked an open-ended question about the types of things they learned about Americans from living with the Volunteer, less than half of respondents mentioned learning about daily life in America or American customs. Responses largely focused on a general work ethic and Americans' informal life style rather than more specific knowledge about

America or Americans. When compared to a standard list of knowledge areas, the most frequent topic about which respondents reported learning—at 51 percent of respondents—was American holidays (Figure 19).

Figure 19: What Host Country Nationals Report Learning from Volunteers: Armenia (n=84)

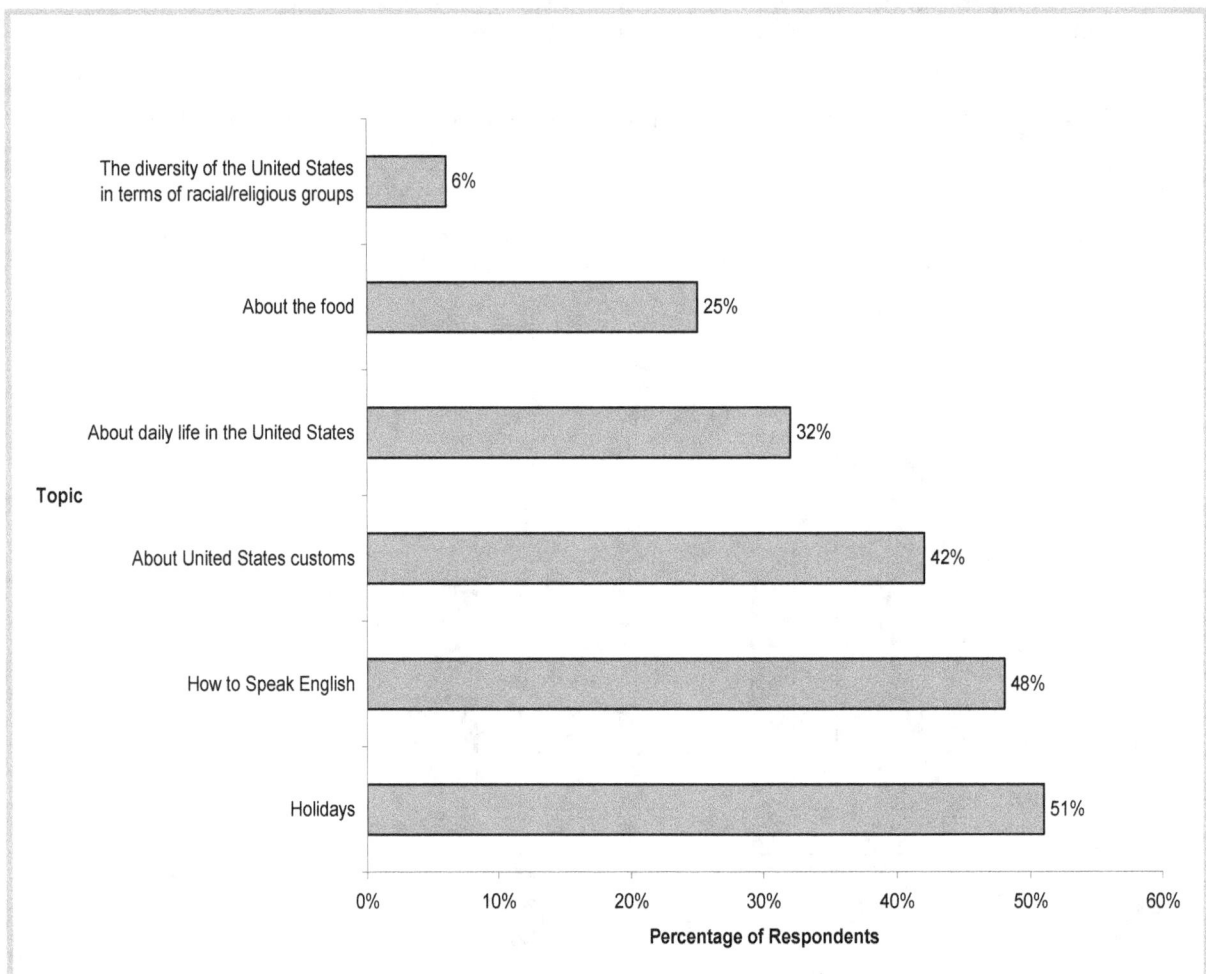

Many responses were positive with regard to more general qualities. Counterparts, for example, found Americans were easy to work with, collaborative, and available for discussions. Students said they learned to appreciate the American approach to life in terms of friendliness and being easy going.

Students also observed that they gained a better understanding of personality traits that they had previously viewed negatively. What was earlier viewed as a cold attitude was now seen as a work-focused attitude, a change demonstrating a potentially more profound understanding of Americans on the part of Armenians. Exchange alumni reported learning most about the patience and the work ethic of Volunteers. They also learned to see the value of Americans' less formal approach to life.

Host family members' opinions of Americans remained mixed. Several reported learning that Americans were less arrogant and less hard–to-please than they previously thought, while others maintained their views that Americans were too informal, ill-behaved, and cold. Due to the small number of NGO staff and ministry officials, and their extensive previous experience with Americans, their responses reflected little change.

What counterparts reported learning about Americans from interacting with a Volunteer:

[I] had some concerns that Americans are difficult, but saw that they are very tolerant. If I were mistaken, I would immediately get help. Very easy-going people.

They are collaborative, able to listen and give advice, ready to help.

[My opinion has] mostly stayed the same. I knew them quite well. The only thing I discovered for myself is that they are friendly.

My attitudes toward them became more positive. Many of their habits can be adopted. They are very patient and self-restrained. I realized that I confused the thoroughness with coldness.

What beneficiaries reported learning about Americans from interacting with a Volunteer:

He was kind and attentive to others, a cheerful person. Now I have to form an opinion about Americans based on his example, but I think people like him are rare in America. He knows how to behave ... he was youthful with children, and mature with the adults.

There are things about them I don't like: they are sometimes overly free; but there are also positive things like being generous, respectful and patriotic.

They do not differ much from us, and they are not that bad; they are simple people, easy-going, intellectual.

Very polite and friendly. Very exacting in work relations, and very friendly outside the school. They are hard workers. They have a minimalist approach to life.

What host family members reported learning about Americans from interacting with a Volunteer:

I couldn't learn anything about USA, because we didn't communicate with them, they were very busy.

How to organize housekeeping and a daily routine, living style and mindset.

I don't know what to think about people from the U.S. We had very different experiences. [Volunteer 1] and [Volunteer 2] were quite different.

Americans are open-minded, easy to communicate with and they treat all people equally regardless of gender, age and social status. They are rather practical people in terms of dressing and daily life.

What exchange alumni reported learning about Americans from interacting with a Volunteer:

I realize that there are different kinds of people. But based on the experience of the PCV I worked with, my perception now is very positive. I hadn't met any other person who can work with such devotion.

They are more communicative, sociable and ingenious than we are. They are really hard workers, but they will always find time for everything. They will never tire you with their problems, and will never let you do so as well.

When asked about the types of things they remembered most about working or living with someone from another country, comments mirrored the responses offered to the previous question about opinions of Americans after interacting with a Volunteer.

Specifically, counterparts recounted stories that demonstrated Volunteers' *caring attitudes and their informal nature*. Beneficiaries and exchange alumni recounted Volunteers' *tolerance* when dealing with uncomfortable situations. Even though host family members reported the least positive views of Americans after interacting with Volunteers, when recounting memorable moments they almost universally focused on positive aspects of Volunteer *enthusiasm and their easy-going attitude*. Only one NGO staff member offered a response to this question. But that response reflects the misunderstanding between the community and the Volunteer that negatively affected the success of the community project.

As reported by the Armenian researchers, 11 percent of the respondents mention that they did not learn anything. In some of the cases, that statement was followed with an explanation that their communication was limited, because the Peace Corps Volunteer was very busy (2 responses). Such answers were mostly provided by host family members. In other cases, respondents stated that they did not get to know anything new, as they had known Americans before (3 responses); two respondents stated that the PCV was trying to learn about Armenia rather than teach. There were four responses by people who did not learn anything, but they were not explained.

Many of the Volunteers provided information to their counterparts and family members about the places they came from—states and the communities, (5 responses) and in some cases about the political system of the United States (4 responses).

The exchange program alumni mentioned that an introduction to the education system and the life of students in the United States was quite useful for them before their departure (4 people) (CDPF, page 48).

What HCNs remember most from interacting with Volunteers

Counterparts:

I was impressed and deeply touched by the card she had made herself and by the thoughts she expressed.

I was impressed one time when he entered the class eating an apple. Students became active and started to ask for apples as well. Later, I told the PCV that this kind of behavior was unacceptable.

Beneficiaries:

Freedom, hard work, being hearty, caring for the environment: once we had a picnic in the forest and the Americans saw how filthy the forest was and initiated cleaning all the waste there.

Her dress was very simple. They do not give too much importance to it and it is of secondary importance for them. I think they are simple at heart as well. They treat everyone equally; they do not rank people high and low as we are doing.

His tolerance also impressed me. Once our students mocked him, he didn't respond the same way; instead he responded [to it] as a joke.

NGO staff:

They come to Armenia like to Africa. They take a position like "we have come to teach you; our way of being is right; yours is wrong". That is why their community activity [has] failed.

Exchange alumni:

I remember the Halloween evening he organized. He periodically organized so- called movie nights. Once we watched a movie on homosexuality and afterwards discussed it. I was surprised how neutrally we discussed such a taboo.

I was surprised that he knew the names of all children and staff of the orphanage and called them all by name.

Host family members:

On New Year's Eve, I put a present under his pillow. When he found it he was so surprised and happy that he was jumping on the bed with joy.

I remember once [the Volunteer's] husband lost his ring while washing. I was extremely upset. He hugged me and said, "in life more serious losses happen."

General Observations from the Armenian Researchers on Armenians' Perceptions of Americans:

Most of the respondents had difficulty or sometimes refused to make generalizations about the Americans. A counterpart stated, "They are very different … in the case of some of them I have changed my opinion, in the case of others I retain my opinion. I have discovered they are a more ingenuous, unconstrained, natural, and benevolent people."

It should be mentioned that, despite the fact that the questions related to Americans in general, the respondents had a hard time separating that general opinion from their experience with one specific Volunteer. The result was that their perception was based on the description of the actual Volunteer. "I realize that there are different kinds of people, but based on the experience of the PCV I worked with, my perception now is much more positive; I had not met any other person, who can work with such devotion." In this context the judgment of a student is worth mentioning: "Now I have to form an opinion about Americans based on his example, but I think people like him are rare in America. He knows how to behave…he treats both children and older people well." Sometimes we can even see elements of idealization of a PCV's personality.

Many beneficiaries expressed balanced views including both positives and negatives: "There are things that I don't like—they are sometimes too free; but there are also positive things like being generous, respectful and patriotic." or "I like that they are well-informed and educated. They are kind, friendly and humanistic. The only thing I didn't like is their lifestyle in terms of hygiene."

It is worth mentioning that in some cases counterparts, beneficiaries, and host family members saw not only positive changes in their attitudes, but also noted their readiness and need to adopt some American habits. Thus, one of the counterparts stated that many of their habits could be adopted. In another case, a respondent praised the rationality of American customs: "I like American culture very much" (CDPF, page 46).

Findings on the Kinds of Terms Respondents Used to Describe Americans

At the end of each interview, the interviewers completed a check list of personality descriptors to indicate whether respondents spontaneously used any of those terms to describe the Volunteer during the interview (Figures 20 and 21).

The most frequently used **positive terms** were:

- Motivated or committed to his or her work (82 percent)
- Hardworking (80 percent)
- Friendly (80 percent)

Most of the **negative terms** were mentioned by less than half of the respondents, with the exception of:

- Unsophisticated (65 percent)
- Individually oriented (58 percent)

- Selfish (50 percent)

Figure 20: Positive Terms Spontaneously Used to Describe Americans: Armenia

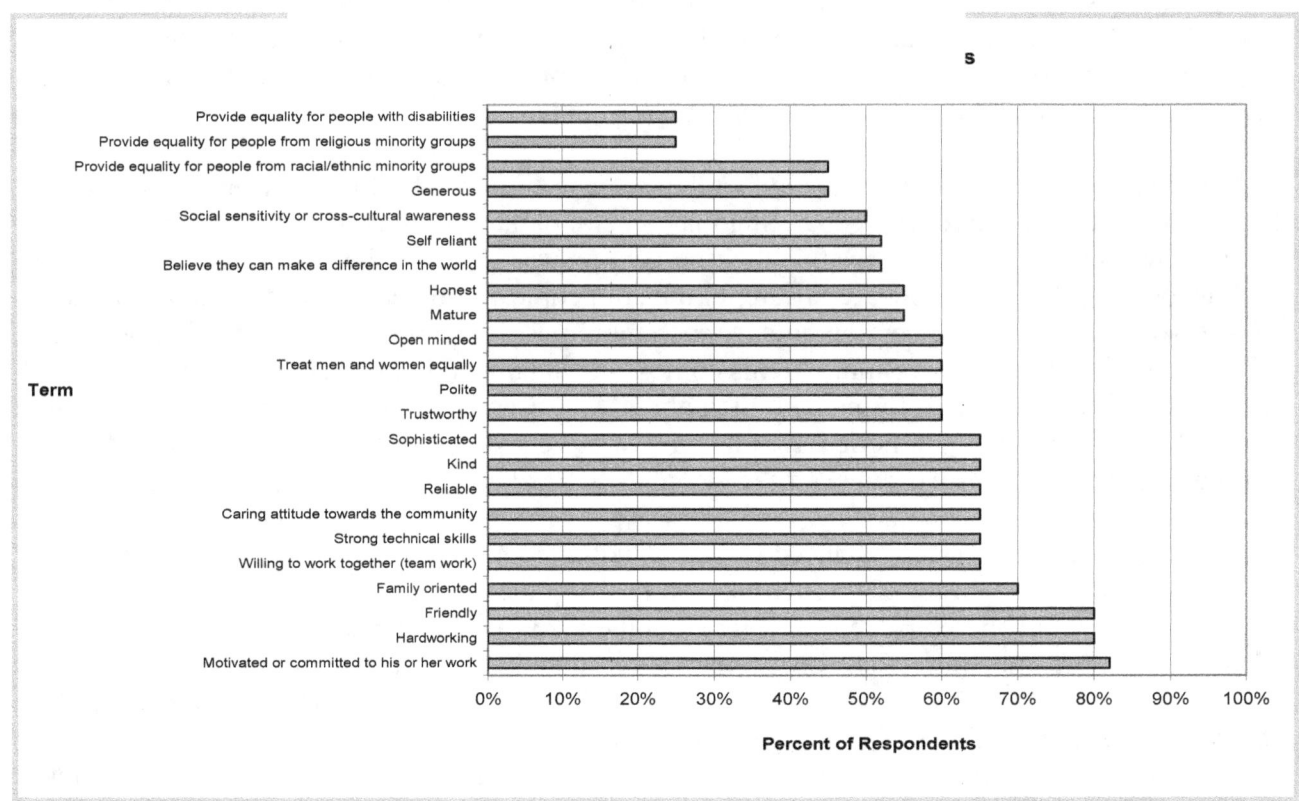

Figure 21: Negative Terms Spontaneously Used to Describe Americans: Armenia

Spontaneously Used Negative Terms to Describe Americans

Term	Percent of respondents
Unreliable	0%
Lacked common sense	0%
Cruel	0%
Impolite	18%
Dishonest	18%
Prejudiced/closed minded	20%
Lazy	22%
Unfriendly	35%
Selfish	50%
Individually oriented	58%
Unsophisticated	65%

Lessons Learned Regarding Goal Two Performance

The following are areas that post staff may want to explore further in order to determine if the findings reflect widespread issues and, if so, how best to address them.

Improving interpersonal relationships: Although host family members indicated that they carried out a range of activities together, 17 percent responded that they were not at all close with the Volunteer they hosted. In addition, there were several comments about the personal habits and cleanliness of the Volunteers, as well as a lack of interest in interacting on the part of the Volunteer. Another, possibly more concerning, aspect of interpersonal relationships is reflected in the comment by an NGO staff member regarding what he remembered most about working with the Volunteer. Specifically, his perception was that the Volunteer was arrogant and looked down on Armenian ways of doing things which reduced the effectiveness of his work.

A decrease in opinion of Americans after hosting a Volunteer: Fourteen percent of host family members reported that their opinion of Americans became more negative as a result of their interactions with a Volunteer.

Limited learning: The main theme in respondents' discussion of what they learned was the Americans' work ethic. Only 32 percent of respondents indicated that they learned about daily life in America and 42 percent learned about American customs.

Volunteers may need to generate more opportunities for sharing information about daily life and American customs. Specific areas for this work can be derived from the terms used by respondents to describe Americans. Specifically, they noted that there should be more focus on teaching about racial/religious and other forms of equality, as well as on cultural and/or social training for Volunteers to avoid being labeled as selfish and unsophisticated. Post may wish to revisit these themes within Pre-Service and In-Service Trainings with Volunteers and Counterparts to explore ways to better understand the cross-cultural interpretations of behaviors.

CONCLUSIONS

Peace Corps meets its goals of building local capacity (Goal 1) and promoting a better understanding of Americans among host country nationals (Goal 2) primarily through the service of its Volunteers. A key element of this service is that Peace Corps Volunteers live in the communities where they work and deliver technical interventions directly to beneficiaries living in areas that often lack local professionals. The impact studies are one way the Peace Corps measures the effect of its Volunteers. In particular, these studies document the HCN perspective on the work of Peace Corps Volunteers.

The data collected in Armenia for Goal 1 indicate that beneficiaries and counterparts improved their English language skills. The teachers adopted the new teaching methods and reported that the capacity building was sustained. Further, respondents were very satisfied with the work of the Volunteers. Some factors were identified which, if addressed, could improve the results achieved. These include: limited class time available for English language instruction and cultural differences (which resulted in a lack of respect for the PCV among students in some cases). More pre-implementation preparation and planning for sustainability would contribute to improved results.

Peace Corps' Goal 2 results were achieved. The majority of HCNs who interacted with Volunteers reported more positive opinions of Americans as a result of working and living with the Volunteers. Armenians most frequently spoke about learning about the Volunteers' work ethic rather than learning specific social or cultural information. While the questions related to Americans in general, the respondents had a hard time separating a general opinion of Americans from their experience with one specific Volunteer. The observations about Americans varied among the different groups interviewed. For example, host family members, who lived with the Volunteers during their first months in country, expressed more negative opinions of their relationships with Volunteers than did counterparts and students. In this case, the intensity of their time together may have exacerbated general cultural misunderstandings. These cultural issues are an area that may merit additional analysis.post may want to explore with their Volunteers and HCNs.

The Peace Corps will continue its efforts to assess its impact and to use the findings to improve operations and programming.

APPENDIX 1: METHODOLOGY[8]

Civic Development and Partnership Foundation was contracted by Peace Corps/Armenia to conduct this study. The following description of the methodology was prepared by the contractors and included in their evaluation report to PC/Armenia.

Evaluation Methodology

The methodological approach for the survey was primarily provided by the Peace Corps and was elaborated and developed during the pre-contract period. This draft methodological report was developed during the first (preparatory) month of the contract period. The information on the impact of Peace Corps was gathered by CDPF, primarily through interviews with people who have lived and worked with Peace Corps Volunteers (PCVs). The following groups were interviewed:

- Host County Nationals (HCN), school based counterparts (team teachers, school administrators, teacher supervisors)

- HCN Non-Governmental Organization (NGO) staff

- Alumni from exchange programs, such as the FLEX, UGrad, and Muskie

- HCN beneficiaries of Peace Corps projects (students of classes taught by PCVs, as well as attendees at camps or events organized by NGOs)

- Host Family members

- Peace Corps Volunteers

The Evaluation Questions

Is the English Language Education Project fulfilling the need for trained people? By measuring the transfer of skills and capacity building of host country counterparts and community members at the macro- level, the questions were designed to find out the following:

1. Are HCNs better trained (i.e., have HCNs increased their knowledge, skills, and/or awareness)?
2. Have those trained improved their ability to meet project goals (i.e., have HCNs altered their behaviors or improved processes and procedures)?
3. Are HCNs satisfied with the Peace Corps' work? Will these changes have a lasting effect? Will the changes remain once the PCV's service has ended (i.e. sustainability)?

---

[8] This section was taken from the research report developed by the in-country research team. As a result the formatting and style vary from those used in the body of the report.

Has the English Language Education Project promoted a better understanding of Americans? By documenting the types of changes in knowledge, attitude, and behavior that host country populations experience through their work and contact with PCVs the questions are designed to find out whether the people who interacted with the Volunteers increased their knowledge and awareness of Americans?

Site Selection and Sampling

Since the study is focused on PC/Armenia's English Language Education Project and its impact during the last five years, the study focused on all English Language Education Project Volunteers who have served or are serving in Armenia starting from the A12 group which arrived in 2004.

The site selection was conducted for the sampling groups to be as representative of Armenia as possible in terms of geographic and socio-economic diversity. Four of Armenia's Marzes (geographical regions) were selected, roughly one from each geographic region: Lori - North, Shirak - West, Syunik - South, and Gegharkunik – East. The selected regions have the most diverse population ranges, including small villages with a population of 600 to larger cities with a population of 150,000. The respondent groups' distribution by regions is presented in the chart below:

Figure 22: Planned and actual distributions of interviews by regions

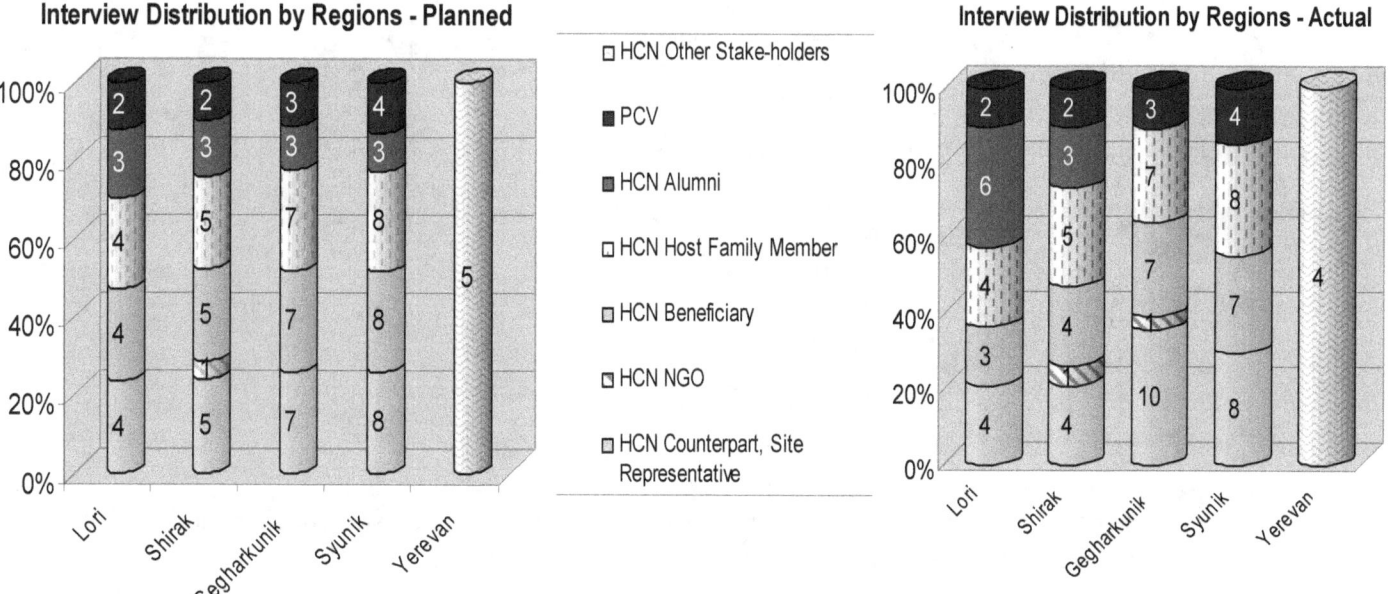

A list of English Language Education Project Volunteers who served in those regions starting in 2004 was generated. The total number of Volunteers that served in the selected regions is 24, out of which 11 PCVs are still in service and 13 have completed their service and were no longer in Armenia during the survey period.

Based on the list of 24 PCVs, other target groups were identified to be interviewed. For each Volunteer, interviews were to be conducted with an HCN counterpart, a site representative, a beneficiary, an alumni, and a host family member. Four or five interviews were planned to be conducted with partner governmental officials as well. The table below shows the planned sample of respondent groups, as well as the actual interviews conducted.

Table 2: Distribution of Respondent Groups: Planned and Actual Sample

	Planned Interviews	Implemented Interviews
HCN Counterpart, Site Representative	24	26
HCN NGO	1	2
HCN Beneficiary	24	21
HCN Host Family Member	24	24
HCN Alumni	12	9
PCV	11	11
HCN Other Stake-holders	4-5	4

In total, 97 respondents were individually interviewed during the survey. The planned respondent groups and the actual distribution in percentages are presented in the charts below.

Figure 23: Planned and actual distribution of interviews by respondent groups

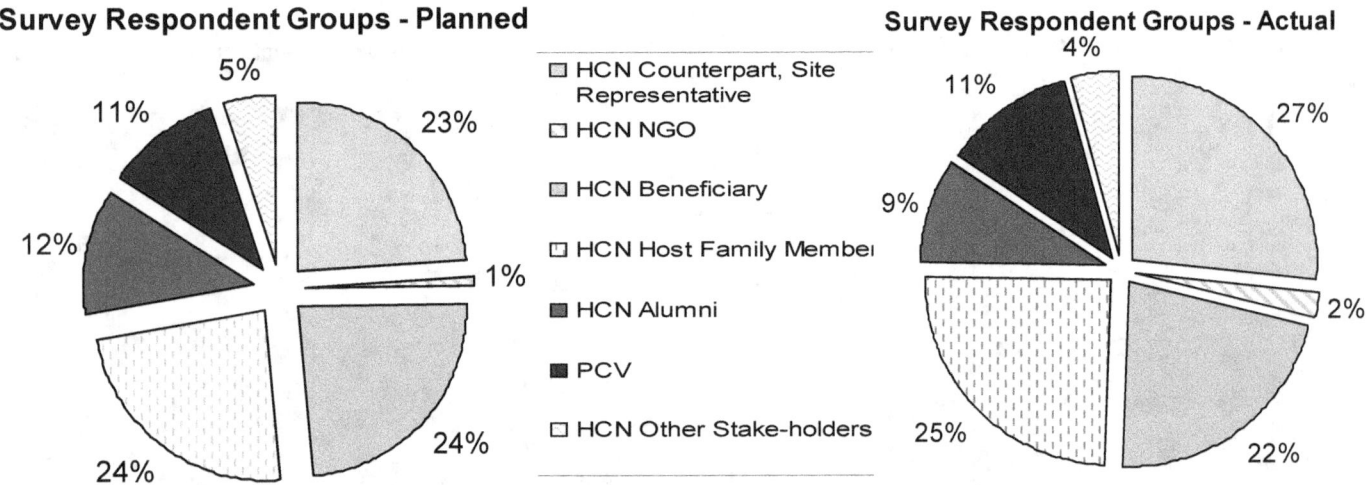

In addition, focus groups were initially planned as an option for selected stakeholders and beneficiaries. The purpose was to summarize the information collected and to get additional clarification and information on selected questions. However, the information collected through interviews was comprehensive enough to reach the necessary conclusions and recommendations. Therefore, conducting the focus groups was considered excessive for the evaluation.

Response Rate

The actual response rate was 96 percent, 97 respondents out of 101 participated in the survey through individual interviews.

Respondent Groups

This section provides a brief overview of each respondent group interviewed. The information gained was helpful in order to interpret the survey findings as well as to generate the conclusions and recommendations.

HCN Counterparts

This group included school based counterparts: team teachers, school administrators, teacher supervisors.

Out of 26 HCN counterparts interviewed, 22 were English language teachers and 4 were school administrators or teacher supervisors. While all the English teachers interviewed were official or non-official counterparts of the PCVs they had

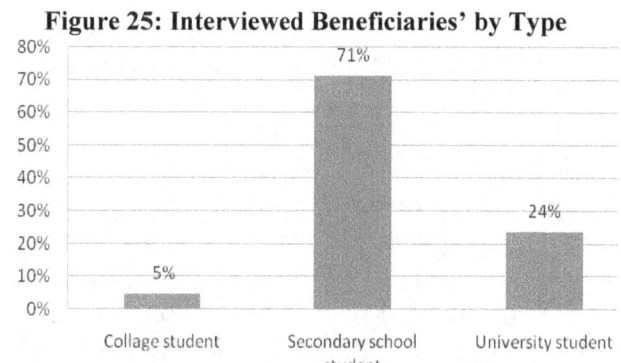

Figure 24: Interviewed Counterparts' Teaching Experience[1]

different experiences working with a PCV and these are elaborated in the findings section of this report. The relative experience of the teachers interviewed is presented in the chart. All the school administrators interviewed had extensive interaction with PCVs and thus contributed to this survey by sharing accumulated experience and providing feedback.

HCN Beneficiaries

This group included beneficiaries of Peace Corps projects: students of classes taught by PCVs, as well as attendees at camps. Overall, 21 beneficiaries were interviewed during the survey. Twenty-four percent of the interviewed beneficiaries were university students, 5 percent beneficiaries interviewed were secondary school students.

Figure 25: Interviewed Beneficiaries' by Type

Overall, the information accumulated from the beneficiaries provided comprehensive data on the questions discussed.

Alumni

This group consisted of alumni of U.S.-sponsored exchange programs such as FLEX, UGrad, and Muskie. Overall, all 9 respondents interviewed provided interesting feedback from various perspectives: 5 alumni had experience working with three or more PCVs, thus the information provided covered a broader experience of working with Peace Corps, rather than just English

Language Education Project Volunteers. The evaluation team considered this fact when analyzing the survey data.

Non-Governmental Organizations

Two NGOs with extensive experience working with Volunteers in their regions were interviewed. One of the NGOs interviewed had experienced working with three Volunteers and the other with 10 Volunteers. Similar to the Alumni group, the respondents had difficulties segregating the accumulated experience, and thus, most of the information provided covers their overall experience of working with Peace Corps and Volunteers.

Host Family Members

Twenty-four host family representatives were interviewed at the sample sites. Fifty-eight percent of the respondents within this group were female (host mothers, host sisters). Twenty-one percent of the interviewed families consisted of two members (the smallest household composition), and the 29 percent were six-member households (the largest). The specifics of household composition (i.e. number of family members, etc.) were considered when the evaluation team interpreted the data.

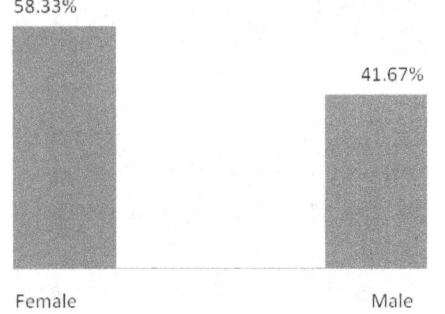

Figure 26: PCVs Gender Distribution Among Host Family Members Interviewed

58.33%

41.67%

Female   Male

Stakeholders

Four stakeholder representatives were interviewed, three of whom were officials from the Ministry of Education and Science, and one from the National Institute of Education. The information generated from the major stakeholder groups interviewed is integrated into the survey findings.

Peace Corps Volunteers

All eleven in-country English Language Education Project Volunteers were interviewed within the survey period: two of them are from A-13, one from A-14, six from A-15 and two from the A-16 group of English Language Education Project Volunteers. While PCVs of groups A13-A15 provided significant contributions in terms of data provision, Volunteers of group A-16 had spent only a month in their sites by the interview period, thus being in the stage of getting familiar with the new environment, they were not very involved in specific activities in the schools and community. All the Volunteers were very helpful in facilitating communications with the HCNs in their sites.

Data Collection

The table below presents the data collection methods in accordance to the research questions:

Research Questions	Data Collection Methods
Are HCNs better trained? Have those trained improved their ability to meet the project goals?	HCN interviews Interviews with PCVs Document/record revision
Are Host Country Nationals satisfied with the work of Peace Corps' English Language Education Project?	HCN interviews Interviews with PCVs Document/record revision
Will the changes have a lasting effect once the PCV's service has ended?	HCN interviews Interviews with PCVs
Have the people who interacted with the Volunteer increased their knowledge and awareness of Americans?	HCN interviews Interviews with PCVs Document/record revision

For all the interviews with the respondent groups, interview protocols developed and provided by the Peace Corps were used.

In addition to the information gathered through interviews, the following secondary data was provided by the Peace Corps and reviewed during data analysis:

- The Memorandum of Understanding between the Peace Corps and the Host Country
- The most recent English Language Education Project Plan and English Language Education Project reports
- Surveys administered to Peace Corps Volunteers including the Returned Peace Corps Volunteer Survey, the Close-of-Service Survey, and the Biennial Volunteer Survey
- Host Country Counterpart surveys
- Field based project reviews

Data Analysis

The survey data was entered into the DatStat online system provided by the Peace Corps. Later, data were converted into SPSS and sent to CDPF for further analysis.

Data analyses were conducted according to the responding group findings and grouping them for each evaluation question. The respondents were combined into the following groups: HCN counterparts, site representatives, beneficiaries, alumni and host family members, as well as major stakeholders (i.e., GOA Ministries). The analysis focused on combining similar findings and presenting those in accordance with the evaluation questions.

Evaluation Team

The Evaluation Team consisted of Senior Researcher Zhirayr Edilyan and two local interviewers, Tatevik Margaryan and Diana Ter-Stepanyan. The local interviewers were responsible for conducting interviews with the main beneficiary groups, as well as entering data into the online system, DatStat. They also participated in data analysis and the development of evaluation recommendations. The senior researcher supervised the field interviews and conducted interviews with key stakeholders. Both the data analysis and the development of the survey reports were facilitated by the senior researcher.

Evaluation Limitations

The following evaluation limitations were inherent in the study design, and were considered when the evaluation team was interpreting the Survey results:

Bias due to respondent's memory or willingness to report: To the extent possible, the interview data gathered was compared to PCVs' responses regarding the extent to which Volunteers think they helped HCNs to gain a better understanding of Americans. Where possible, respondents' information about how and whether they think that the PCV affected their understanding of Americans and others was compared within subgroups of related respondents and examined for trends.

Measurement of broad concepts: The concepts of meeting host country's needs and promoting a better understanding of Americans are so broad that they do not have standard definitions. Further, there are no universally accepted valid and reliable measures of these concepts. As a result, the data gathered through these interviews is exploratory rather than confirmatory.

Measuring short term outcomes: Changes in attitudes, knowledge, and awareness are typically short term project outcomes. Changes in behaviors and practices may be intermediate outcomes. These interviews made it possible to gather information about attitude, awareness, and knowledge changes (i.e., short term outcomes) related to both strategic goals. Where possible, secondary data, including project records, was used to compile information about long term capacity building outcomes.

In addition, the following technical limitations have also been revealed during the preparation, field work, and data analysis stages and should be considered accordingly:

Protocol finalization and adjustment: In accordance with the training of researchers and contract conditions, the evaluation team was to receive the draft interview protocols, and translate and adjust them for all the respondent groups (the only protocol drafted by the CDPF was one for stakeholder interviews). The communication and negotiation processes were carried out with some difficulties and suffered from significant delays according to the initially developed survey timelines, both of which caused additional delays in implementing the other planned activities, including field work and data analysis. Another technical problem was that due to the volume of protocols, the data analysis took more time than was initially planned.

Correlations of various data: The information generated contained very detailed background information on respondents, such as the number of PCVs they worked/lived with, the duration of time spent working/living with PCVs, the number of years in position, etc. Considering the appropriateness of the evaluation questions set, this type of information is and provided in the report. Nevertheless, the sample of each respondent group was very limited in number, and thus the generated correlation coefficients in data analyses are not statistically significant in most cases.

Objectivity of respondents' judgment: The interview protocols for all the respondent groups contain comparative questions about respondents' understanding of Americans before working/living with PCVs. The interview process showed that respondents had difficulties while answering these kinds of questions, since the generated experience of working with a PCV had had a significant influence on the HCNs mindset in most of the cases. While interpreting the data generated, the evaluation team tried to consider this circumstance while providing the evaluation findings.